DEM☉S

Demos is an independent think tank committed to radical thinking on the long term problems facing the UK and other advanced industrial societies.

It aims to develop ideas – both theoretical and practical – to help shape the politics of the 21st century, and to improve the breadth and quality of political debate.

Demos publishes books and a quarterly journal and undertakes substantial empirical and policy oriented research projects. Demos is a registered charity.

In all its work Demos brings together people from a wide range of backgrounds in business, academia, government, the voluntary sector and the media to share and cross-fertilise ideas and experiences.

For further information and
subscription details please write to:
Demos
9 Bridewell Place
London, EC4V 6AP
Telephone: 0171 353 4479
Facsimile: 0171 353 4481
email: mail@demos.co.uk

First published in 1997 by
Demos
9 Bridewell Place
London EC4V 6AP
Telephone: 0171 353 4479
Facsimile: 0171 353 4481
email: mail@demos.co.uk
© Demos 1997

Paper No. 26
ISBN 1 898309 48 5
Printed in Great Britain by
EG Bond Ltd
Designed by Esterson Lackersteen
Illustrations by Damien Cranny
Typeset by Lindsay Nash
Thanks to Adrian Taylor

Contents

Acknowledgements

The writing of this book was a collaborative effort and a model of teamwork among women and men. We are particularly indebted to Geoff Mulgan, the Director of Demos, for his ideas, advice and editorial assistance. Sarah Gregory, Helen Hayes and Rowena Young, all of whom work at Demos, not only helped to research aspects of this report, but also contributed to the development of the ideas. Thanks, too, to Ben Reason who designed the graphs and tables, to Damien Cranny, our cartoonist, and to Lindsay Nash, our Publications Manager, who typeset this report under harsh time constraints with great efficiency. We are grateful to the Henley Centre who gave us permission to draw on their Planning for Social Change programme and for giving us permission to publish their data. Finally we owe a special debt of thanks to Pat Dade, Managing Director of Synergy Brand Values, who not only acted as a consultant in the preparation of this report but who analysed the *Insight '96* survey for the first time publicly. Naturally for all those involved the usual disclaimers apply.

Helen Wilkinson and Melanie Howard, February 1997

Summary

This century has brought more profound changes to women's lives than any previous period in human history. Women make up a majority of the electorate and will soon make up a majority of the workforce, even though most of our institutions, from Parliament to big employers, have yet to adapt to this new reality.

If current trends continue, women in 2010 will be: more numerous (there are already 1.2 million more women than men in Britain); older (by 2030 a quarter of women will be over 65); more independent (a fifth of women born in the 60s are predicted to remain childless); more likely to be living alone (a third of all households will be single by 2010); more likely to be divorced (40 per cent of marriages are predicted to end in divorce); more likely to be in management or the professions (52 per cent of new solicitors and 32 per cent of managers and administrators are women); more dependent on technologies ranging from intelligent tags to mobile phones; more androgynous (31 per cent of women are now at ease with flexible gender roles); more likely to be from an ethnic minority (up from 6 per cent to 9 per cent); and better educated, with a third of each new age cohort going through university.

However, a linear extrapolation of current trends can be misleading. As we show, the interaction of the many different forces shaping women's lives could block their long march to equality; gaps in pay and opportunities could widen once again; the frustration experienced by many less skilled women could explode; and a return of traditional values could push women back into the home.

To provide insights into the likely shape of women's lives in 2010, this report draws on two major new surveys of women's values – by AGB Taylor Nelson and Synergy – that have involved interviews with a representative sample of over 3000 women from across Britain, on Demos, and the Future Foundation's own studies of changing demography, labour markets, technology and values, and on the Henley Centre's Planning for Social Change programme. This summary sets out some of the key findings.

Society is becoming more feminine

As male jobs disappear, women's importance in society is set to rise, as is their confidence. Forty per cent of women believe that women are naturally superior to men. Women will soon make up a majority of the workforce and Britain is becoming increasingly shaped by feminine values. Values such as empathy and care, community and environmentalism, are now central to British society. Older values associated with authority, the military, and the traditional family have been displaced. Work has become more important for women, and nearly all groups of women have become relatively less committed to the family over the last ten years. While women have made inroads into previously male fields like the professions and the police, and into sports such as mountaineering, men have become more concerned about health and appearance and have begun to organise themselves as victims of educational and jobs failure, and discrimination.

No feminism, only feminisms

Tomorrow's women will be more different from each other than women are today – in terms of life experience, opportunities and values. There will be no women's movement - only women's movements, no feminism, only feminisms. We predict the rise of business feminism, trade union feminism, new age feminism – but their adherents will not have any automatic sense of solidarity with each other. Only 15 per cent of women now define themselves primarily by gender, fewer than define themselves by their intelligence. Although women are becoming more assertive, they are unlikely to coalesce into a single movement, and politicians, advertisers and businesses will find it increasingly hard to appeal to a 'typical' woman.

Frustration explodes?
Feminism has led to a mushrooming of frustrated ambition among a younger generation, particularly in single women. Millions of women in less skilled jobs have heightened expectations which aren't being met. Fifteen per cent of all women (3.6 million) say that they are getting a raw deal out of life, and 23 per cent (5.6 million) say that they feel angry much of the time – mainly younger women in classes D and E. Overall, 60 per cent of women say that employers are still prejudiced. We predict a harder, less compromising feminism in the workplace in the future as frustrated women learn to organise. After all, for most women in part-time, insecure jobs, the glass ceiling is irrelevant; the key is to achieve time flexibility, more security, more training and higher pay.

Traditionalism returns?
The back to basics movement is likely to gain growing support, even though it is now primarily supported by over 55s. Partly because of inadequate opportunities at work, and partly because of anxieties about childcare, growing numbers of women will want to be at home. Thirteen per cent (3.2 million) of women are working but would rather be at home – most of them under 35. Thirty-six per cent of 25 to 34 year old women believe that family life suffers if a woman works full time. We could see the

evolution of a 'cult of motherhood', and a new 'mum's movement', bolstered by new agers who choose opting out to have a family over clinging to the career ladder.

Women becoming like men

We predict the flourishing of a new generation of mannish women who will ape men's traditional behaviour by hiring male escorts and male secretaries, enjoying the power they can exert over them. They will be more hedonistic, assertive and risk taking. They will spend ever less time on house cleaning, accepting male standards of cleanliness. Thirty-one per cent of women say that they would not mind being born again as a man. The proportion of women knitting or dressmaking has fallen by 10 per cent while the proportion doing DIY has risen from 24 to 30 per cent over the course of the last decade. 16-24 year old women's smoking has gone up 5 per cent since 1994. A quarter of football fans are now women. Women are even becoming physically more like men – with an increase in heart disease, serotonin levels and drinking, as physical consequences of their changing lifestyle. Men by contrast may be set to take over from women as the main pill poppers, suffering more from depression. They may also have other reasons to be worried. As 17 per cent of women say they 'don't get mad, they get even', we are likely to see more women in the vein of Lorena Bobbit and Sharon Stone's ice pick wielding killer in *Basic instinct*.

New agers on the rise

Women are becoming increasingly attached to new age values, alternative therapies, and spirituality. Twenty-six per cent of all women say that they 'feel part of a world spirit'. Thirty-six per cent say that the most important decisions in their lives are based on emotions. Balance is becoming a general concern and environmentalism is now mainstream, at the core of British values overall. The 'new age' women, who are generally more affluent, will increasingly educate their children at home, opt out of career ladders, and provide potential allies for 'back to basics' women in championing a less work-oriented culture. However, we predict that 'downshifting' will remain relevant only to a small minority – and mainly at particular lifestages.

Flexibility and time rise up the agenda

Britain has seen a revolution in women's work – but the main institutions have failed to adapt. Forty-eight per cent of working women say that flexible working hours are their highest priority, but only a small minority of employers offer such options as term-time working and four day weeks. Eighty-six per cent of working women say that they never have time to get things done. There are only 600 workplace nurseries. We predict much bigger political pressures around issues such as parental leave and childcare, which are now largely off the political agenda in the UK in stark contrast to other countries.

Stuck in the technology ghetto?

Women are in danger of being trapped in a technology ghetto. They are significantly less confident with technology than men, and see technologies like the PC and Internet as less relevant to their lives. Only 33 per cent of women use computers at work compared to 47 per cent of men. Only 20 per cent of women see the Internet as useful, and only 4 per cent of women use the Internet at work compared to 15 per cent of men.

Women and business

Twice as many new businesses are being set up by women as by men, rapidly transforming Britain's small business culture. But women are mainly going into business for freedom. Only 15 per cent say they do it for the money, compared to 34 per cent who do it for fulfilment. But all is not rosy for women in business. Fifty-six per cent of women managers suffer from ill health because they don't have time for exercise or a good diet. Women are becoming very cynical about companies. Sixty per cent of women over 35 are angry at companies telling lies and acting unethically. Working women in particular have become significantly more sceptical about companies over the last decade.

Women doing without men

Looking further ahead, the continued fall in the sperm count and the continuing 'oestrogen storm' mean that men's fertility will continue to fall. Coupled with medical innovations to control conception, pregnancy and birth, the implication is that by early in the next century women won't need men to produce babies.

Things that matter

The three factors that women cite as having had most influence on their lives this century are the pill, the right to vote, and the washing machine, in that order. Looking ahead to 2010, we might expect a women's football league on mainstream television, a 'mothers' movement' with millions of members, DIY pregnancy kits as well as DIY pregnancy tests, a new generation of women cyberbillionaires, an army of 'femocrats' gaining ground in government and quangos, the first major counter-demonstration by women against a men's movement march, and a new generation of smart clothes that tell washing machines how to wash them and smart food products that instruct ovens how to cook them.

More political women?

So far women have failed to mobilise their new power at work and as consumers. Part of the reason is that their interests diverge. Their energies have been directed much more to private life and work. But we predict that over the next dozen or so years they will become more assertive. Far from feminism disappearing into a depoliticised 'post-feminism' we anticipate more politicisation in the future – whether among older traditionalist women with time on their hands campaigning against abortion or pornography, or among younger women frustrated about lack of opportunities or angry about the environment.

The end of 'men-only politics'?

We also predict that women will become more prominent in mainstream politics. Women are a majority of the electorate, and they vote more than men. But they are not happy about how the parties treat them. Seventy-five per cent of 25 to 54 year old women are dissatisfied with the parties' records on women's issues. Indeed, 1997 could be the last general election when the agenda has been almost entirely set by men. A sharp increase in the number of women MPs in 1997, combined with growing numbers of women on local councils, in the media and business will make women much more visible in British public life. By 2010 the 'men-only' agenda of contemporary British politics will be a thing of the past.

The long march to equality

Introduction

Women have come a long way in the last two decades. Britain has seen its first woman prime minister come and go, the appointment of the first woman chief executive of a FTSE top one hundred company, steady advances by women in the workplace, in the professions and in business, and a continuing spread of feminist values throughout the population. At a global level, women's issues have been put firmly on the international agenda, through events like the United Nations Beijing conference.

These shifts have been the culmination of a century that has brought greater change to women's lives than any other period in human history. Changes as diverse as the advent of the contraceptive pill and the washing machine, the achievement of suffrage and the passing of equality laws, have transformed the experiences and status of women. And while at the beginning of this century only half of all 30 year old women, and less than a third of 30 year olds with children, were in work, today more than two-thirds are. In the last decade alone 1.3 million women have joined the labour force.[1]

Women have gained ground in fields where they were

previously almost invisible. Jenny Saville, Mona Hatoum and Rachel Whiteread in the visual arts, Karren Brady managing director of Birmingham City FC, in sport; Beeban Kidron and Meera Syal in film; Deborah Warner and Ruth Mackenzie in theatre; Bunty Mathias in dance; Vivienne Westwood in fashion; and Rosie Boycott and Bridget Rowe in newspapers. Others have made inroads in more traditionally male fields like Pauline Clare, the first chief constable, Yvonne Kershaw the first woman to pilot a Boeing 747, the sailor Lisa Clayton, and the cosmonaut Helen Sharman.

Each of these women has blazed a trail for the next generation. But in spite of these dramatic changes, what the future holds is less clear. Will we see the long march towards equality, towards parity for women in institutions like Parliament and the judiciary, and in the boardroom continue? Or will other forces push in the opposite direction, driving women back into the home?

At the end of the 1990s the signals are mixed. On the one hand, equal opportunities are supported across the political spectrum and deep-rooted economic shifts appear to be benefiting women. On the other hand, anxieties about the effects of careers on children, backlashes on issues such as abortion, barriers in the labour market and the financial pressures on the welfare state because of an ageing society could all halt the forward march, just as past periods of advance for women have often been followed by periods of retreat.

This report provides a way of thinking about women's possible futures. It sets out the major trends – in demographics, economics, technology, organisational capital, politics and values. And it describes five types of woman – already discernible today – whose lives offer prisms for thinking about the opportunities and dilemmas British women will face over the next few years.

We don't claim to predict the future. No one can. But the story told in this report suggests that there is a strong likelihood that tomorrow's women will be even more different from each other than today's women. We forecast a growing divergence between the successful and the unsuccessful, between single women and those in relationships, between women with children and those without, between the highly educated and the less educated, between different generations of women and between the values of the leading edge and those of the traditionalists. We predict that in turn these will make it harder than ever for politics and business to deal with women as a homogeneous block.

The book draws on Demos' methodology, Serious Futures, described in the appendix which accompanies this report. We also have the unique advantage of being able to draw on a mass of time trends data, published here for the first time, from Synergy Brand Values Limited, from the AGB Taylor Nelson/Future Foundation *Changing lives* survey, from MORI, from the Henley Centre and from other original research by Demos.

As this book makes clear, nothing is preordained. The future for women will be shaped more than anything by their own choices and the different ways in which they can be active rather than passive. This report is, we hope, a tool to that end, a means for helping women to make choices and to realise a better future.

Demography as a driver: more life for women outside traditional family and childbearing structures

We begin with demographics. Although more boys than girls are born each year, there are 1.2 million more women than men in Britain.[2] On average women live five years longer than men.[3] By 2010 women will form an even larger majority than they do today. Forecasters expect sharp rises in the numbers of very elderly women: by 2030 a quarter of all women will be over 65 and one in eight will be over 75.[4] As with men there is a marked population bulge made up of baby boomers now aged between 35 and 55. Although Britain has already done most of its ageing by comparison with countries like Japan and Germany, it is still likely that in 2010, the financial and care pressures of an ageing society will be falling on women. By then, men's and women's retirement ages will be converging: the government has promised that by 2020 state retirement ages will have been equalised.

At the other end of the age range there may be fewer young women being born. Women's fertility rates declined from a peak of 2.95 in 1964 to a low point of 1.69 in 1977.[5] Since then the rate has levelled off. Almost a fifth of women born since the 1960s are predicted to remain voluntarily childless,[6] partly because work and careers are being valued more highly than motherhood. In terms of family life, women are marrying later,[7] having children later and are choosing to have fewer of them,[8] partly because of the long term effects of improvements in contraception that have given women control over reproduction. Average 'completed family size' fell from 2.22 for women born in 1945 to a forecast figure of only 1.80 for women born in 1975.[9] This means that the generations born after 1950 are not having enough children to maintain the population, although the effects of this will not be apparent for another 30 years.

Women increasingly cohabit outside of marriage,[10] and more are opting for the single life. One report predicted that by 2011 there would be 3.1 million bachelors and spinsters in England alone, three times the number in 1971.[11] By 2010, the proportion of single households is forecast to be 34 per cent, a third of whom will be women over 60.[12] Average household size will continue to shrink. It has already declined from an average of four in 1900 to 2.72 in 1981 and only 2.48 in 1991.[13]

One of the factors is family breakdown. Between 1961 and 1991 divorces rose six-fold, and 40 per cent of marriages are predicted to end in divorce, and people are divorcing sooner. Over 70 per cent of breakups are now initiated by women. In general, higher divorce rates tend to reflect greater financial independence for women.[14]

Another dimension of demographics is geography. Choice of location will continue to influence women's prosperity. Younger women are continuing to move into the big cities, often because of higher education, with concomitant rises in social status, but many also move out of the city to start families. When they do so, they suffer a sharp decline in their socio-economic status which their male partners avoid.[15] Meanwhile, many older women live in small towns and rural areas and are dependent on public transport services which have deteriorated in recent years.

British women will also reflect other shifts, such as the doubling in the proportion of people from ethnic minorities, from about six per cent today to roughly one in ten by the early decades of the next century.[16]

Taken together, all these factors mean that women now and in the future will spend less of their lives engaged in the traditional female roles of housewife and mother. They will spend more time outside the home and on their own – *potentially* determining their own lives.

Economics as a driving force

Women have become big players in the economy partly because of deep rooted changes in the British economy over the past few decades. The decline of manufacturing and the rise of the service economy have propelled women into the workforce.[17] The proportion of women as a percentage of the total workforce rose from 35 per cent in 1960 to 49 per cent in 1993.[18] In just five years' time women will be in the majority in employment in the UK, constituting 51 per cent of employees.[19]

Higher educated groups of women have benefited the most from this expansion and their advance within the professions looks almost irreversible: 52 per cent of new solicitors, 32 per cent of managers and administrators, 34 per cent of health professionals, and 27 per cent of buyers, brokers and sales representatives are women.[20] Professional jobs are growing faster than any other occupational group, and women are forecast to fill around 44 per cent of all professional posts by 2001.[21]

Young women have been the main beneficiaries. There

are already more female professionals under 35 – 58 per cent – than over that age.[22] The typical professional woman is therefore young, while the typical professional man is older. And there are now more female solicitors under 30 than male ones.[23] The fact that girls are outperforming boys in schools and at universities also means that among today's teenagers, women have closed the education gap and are in fact more qualified now than their male counterparts.[24]

Women are gradually making inroads into the corridors of power. There are more women who are directors of companies and sitting on boards of top companies than ever before.[25] They are also creating opportunities for themselves; during the 1980s, women's self-employment rose by 81 per cent compared with 51 per cent for men and one in four of all self-employed people are women.[26]

The dramatic growth in women's employment is partly a product of the increase in part-time work. The number of women in part time work has risen by a million in the past decade and women now make up 85 per cent of this workforce.[27] Part-time work has traditionally been low in pay and prestige, but this is beginning to change as the rights of part-time workers are codified[28] (partly by the courts) and as more flexible working patterns gain acceptance further up the hierarchy. Seven out of ten blue chip companies now employ part-time managers and over 80 per cent of employers believe that part-time working for managers will become increasingly popular.[29]

Motherhood has become less of a barrier to work than it once was. Nearly half of married and cohabiting women with pre-school children are working today compared with just one quarter fifteen years ago.[30] This trend accelerated rapidly in the 1980s. Employment rates among women with children grew faster during this period than among women without children, and half of the employment growth for mothers was in full-time work.[31] Moreover, between 1985 and 1991 the UK experienced one of the fastest rises of employment growth in the European Union among women with children under ten; a growth which came equally from full- and part-time work.[32] As significant in the long run is the fact that employment among mothers with a child under five grew by 77 per cent compared to only 9 per cent for mothers with children aged 11 to 15 years.[33] As female breadwinning has become more central to the family economy so too the opportunity costs of leaving the labour market have risen. Indeed women who take advantage of job protected maternity leave are less likely to suffer from the 'family gap', the pay gap that widens when women have children.[34]

Women's enhanced role in the economy means that they have begun to benefit from, and gain access to, greater wealth. Women are no longer providers of 'pin money'. The number of women earning more than their partners has trebled from one in fifteen in the early 1980s to one in five in 1995.[35] Among childless couples with degrees, for example, women now provide nearly half (48 per cent) of the household income.[36]

These are all positive indicators of progress. But do they tell the whole story? Alongside steady advances for many women, there has also been a growing divergence between the haves and have-nots, the ins and the outs. And while inequality has widened in society as a whole, women have tended to be on the losing rather than the winning side, even though a large minority have done very well. Since less than a million women work in the professions, for the great majority arguments about glass ceilings are largely irrelevant; they are more concerned about slow and steady progress than about breaking into the boardroom.

The growth in women's employment has largely taken place in less secure parts of the labour market. There has been very little change in the proportion of women working full time. Instead, the big growth of part-time work in the 1950s and 1960s has continued, with 43 per cent of women working part time compared to only 6 per cent of men.[37] For most women part-time work is a choice.

Average gross weekly earnings in the UK

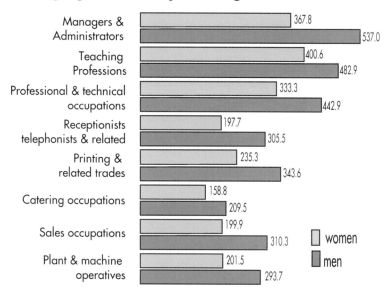

Source: *New earnings survey*, 1995.

But one of the effects of this choice has been to slow the narrowing of the pay gap between men and women, and as this chart shows there remains a substantial gap in widely varying occupations.

Why is pay still unequal twenty years after equal opportunities legislation? The main contributing factors are the following:

● Although the pay gap has narrowed among the youngest age groups (it is only 15 per cent for 16 to 24 year olds compared to 23 per cent for women as a whole), women still run into a 'family gap' with their pay falling relative to men by as much as one third when they have children.[38]

● Most of the growth in jobs has been in part-time, non permanent and contract work[39] – areas which are insecure and poorly paid and where employers are unwilling to invest much in training.

● Women are often in discontinuous employment, moving rapidly in and out of part-time work or self-employment and they change jobs more often than men. Forty per cent of men have been with their employer for more than ten years compared to less than 20 per cent of women with children.[40]

● Women still occupy only a tiny minority of management positions[41] while they provide the majority of the workforce in the poorly paid caring professions.

● Women are negotiating these barriers with little support for their family life. There is little state supported childcare and Britain has been slow to adopt more generous schemes for maternity and parental leave.

The Equal Opportunities Commission has shown that pay inequality worsens with age and type of employment. Part-time women workers earn less than half the pay of men in full-time employment doing the same work – and it is here that most of the employment gains for women have been achieved. Many organisations have increased their use of fixed term contracts. In one study, 50 per cent of organisations had increased their use of fixed term contracts, 60 per cent reported more use of temporary and casual work, and 50 per cent more use of part-timers.[42]

Single mothers face even more difficulties, and as many as half are now without a job. Becoming involved in the means of production has failed to deliver power to many women. There are still both objective and subjective barriers – which is why according to the Henley Centre, 60 per cent of women believe that many employers are still prejudiced against women.

Women as consumers
As consumers, women may have more power than they realise. Women have long been more confident and capable purchasers of basic household items and food than men, largely due to experience. While this pattern is changing and men are taking on more of the responsibility for household purchases, the *Changing lives* research shows that women are less dependent on name brands, more able to make informed choices and more

Men continue to be more attached than women to branded goods

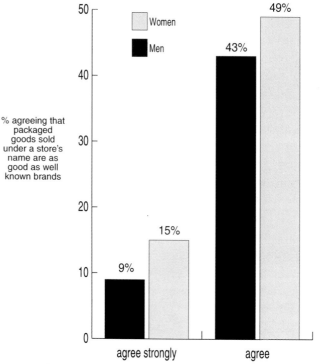

Source: *Changing lives 1996*, AGB Taylor Nelson/Future Foundation, London.

likely to be happy to buy own label products than men. Women also bring other factors into their choices as consumers than men, whether these are environmental concerns, concerns about the ethics of companies, their trading policies (with Tesco's recent adoption of the Trade Fair campaign a telling decision), or community involvement (where companies like BT have invested considerable effort). As we shall see, working women have become strikingly sceptical about companies. But so far, this consumer power has not been translated into active campaigning on issues like equal opportunities.

Control over reproduction
One of the biggest drivers of change in recent decades has been control over reproduction. The advent of the pill

and legal access to abortion were key. But further extensions of reproductive capability are creating difficult new ethical dilemmas; how they are resolved could play an important part in shaping women's lives. 1996 brought good examples of the type of issue that is likely to become more common, with the well publicised cases of Mandy Allwood (pregnant with eight babies) and Diane Blood (who has been given the right to be impregnated with her dead husband's sperm). In the near future the potential to fertilise and nurture embryos away from the human body will transform perceptions of parenthood, as will the wider availability of genetic information produced by the Human Genome Project. At the same time, the abortion debate has returned to the UK, as it has in the US, where abortion clinics are subject to bomb attacks. There is still overwhelming public support for rights to abortion – a MORI poll for the National Abortion Campaign found 81 per cent in favour of a woman's right to choose[43] – but anti-abortion campaigners are becoming more confident.

While growing control over female fertility should be good news for women, the other big trend is declining male fertility. A Finnish study published in the *British Medical Journal* revealed a drop from 56.4 per cent in 1981 to 26.9 per cent in 1991 in the percentage of men capable of normal sperm production.[44] The consequences of global male infertility have been fictionalised by PD James in her book *Children of men*, written when this decline was first noticed in 1992. Women may no longer be able to assume that fertile sperm will be available when they decide to reproduce – rendering them less dependent on their immediate male partner, but also perhaps making them more anxious about parenthood in general.

Technology: affirmative action needed to avoid the electronic ghetto?

Governments around the world now see it as a key policy goal to speed up the adoption of new technologies. But technologists have always been slow to understand women's needs, and women themselves have tended to be slow to adopt new technologies – seeing PCs and the Internet as 'toys for the boys'. There is now a significant technology gap between men and women that could become more significant during a period of rapid technological change.

Less access and experience
The Future Foundation's study for the DMA and Informix – *The new information trade*[45] – found that current regular use of most new technologies was consistently lower at work and at home for women. Even women's use of computers in the workplace is significantly lower than

Women already in the electronic ghetto

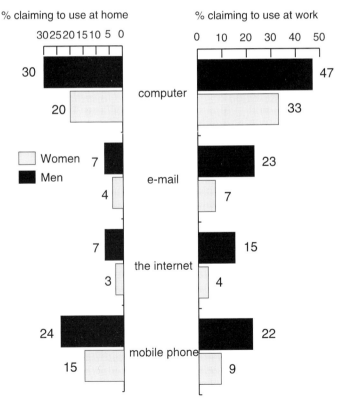

% claiming to use at home   % claiming to use at work

Source: *The new information trade*, DMA/Informix, London, 1996.

men's, standing at 33 per cent compared to 47 per cent. Experience with the Internet is still limited to a small minority of both sexes, with a sharp gender gap.

Lower interest and enthusiasm levels
The DTI's recent research for their 'IT for All' campaign by MORI shows how, in a sample of 3,000 adults, women are less impressed with everything but the mobile phone. Fewer than 20 per cent saw the Internet as useful compared to over 30 per cent of men.

How useful are new technologies?

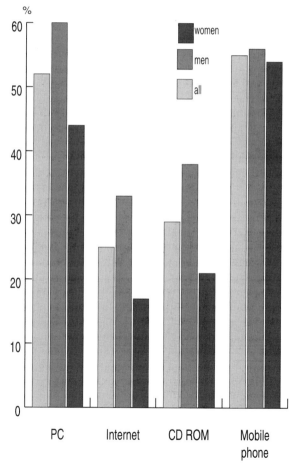

Source: *IT for all*, Department of Trade and Industry, London, 1996.

Older women in particular don't have access and experience
All the demographic indicators for the 'electronic ghetto' are predictable: the old, the poor and women are less knowledgeable about every new development. Smart cards, into which Demos is currently undertaking research funded by the ESRC, are a good case in point: men are twice as likely as women to know what a smart card is.[46] Looking ahead there may be a danger that women will find it harder to access information, particularly if some public information currently available in print becomes available only over the Internet.

Demographic indicators on smart card knowledge

% claiming to know
what a smart card is

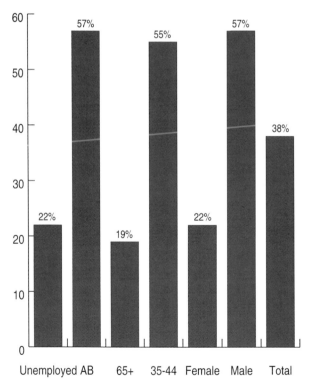

Source: *The new information trade*, DMA/Informix, London, 1996.

One might imagine that women would be eager to learn about new technologies to overcome their disadvantage and to achieve more flexibility in working and parenting. However, active adoption remains the privilege of an affluent and professional minority of women. When the 'battle for the living room' – between PCs and television – hots up, this could prove significant. As major consumers of media, particularly in print form, women may be more resistant to new forms of access and information provision. Certainly among older age groups, more will be at ease accessing services through the TV screen than with a PC and modem.

The challenge for policy makers is to motivate all women to become technologically literate rather than just

Women are less concerned about their safety and security

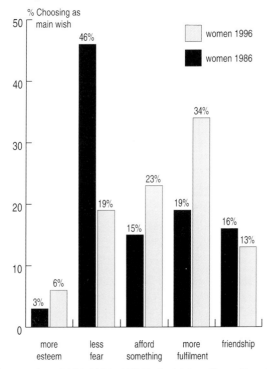

Source: *Changing lives 1986-1996*, AGB Taylor Nelson/Future Foundation, London.

waiting for the generation now passing through schools. The idea of a 'driving licence' for computers is being mooted within the European Union, and could simplify acquisition of the necessary skill[47] – but on its own it will do nothing to address the gender gap.

Another aspect of technological developments which has favoured women in the past and will continue to do so in the future is the development of time saving devices for housework, cooking and washing. One important harbinger of the future is the advent of 'intelligent' tags combining a tiny radio transmitter and a microchip, which eventually will be able to create the TV dinner that cooks itself and the label that tells the washing machine which cycle to use. Houses could be equipped with an 'intelligent' larder which would interrogate the groceries and re-order the ones which have reached their sell-by date or are in short supply.

Technology such as CCTV, mobile phones and stun guns has enhanced women's sense of their personal safety. Partly as a consequence, women are less afraid than they were ten years ago as the chart opposite from the *Changing lives* data shows.

Women lead in the talking stakes

Interestingly, women are leaders in their use of a technology that has become so central and accepted in our daily lives that it has all but 'disappeared' – the telephone. Benefiting from strengths in sociability and communication skills, women use the phone more, enjoy it more and are generally more confident about using it.[48] The next chart shows that the enjoyment 'divide' has increased slightly despite BT's advertising aimed at getting men to make more 'small talk'.[49]

Given that the telephone is still the only truly popular interactive communications tool available to the British public and will continue to have higher rates of penetration (currently some 92 per cent of households) well into the next millennium, this is an advantage worth having. It is reflected in the high proportion of women

Women enjoy using the telephone more than men

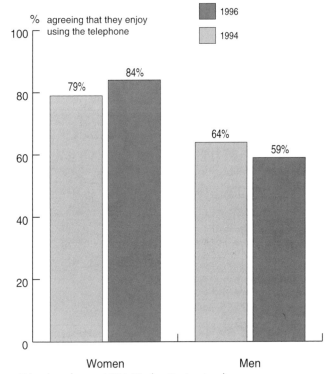

Source: *Teleculture futures 1996*, Henley Centre, London.

providing customer service over the telephone, in the growing number of call centres, and it contributes to the relative success of professional women in freelancing and networking in communications and professional industries. It is also the reason why women have adopted mobile telephones with enthusiasm, both as private individuals and professionally. The trend to providing mobile communications (as pagers or phones for the more affluent) to teenagers is suggestive of just how important telecoms could become for holding families together in the future. Keeping in touch with children at home is the thrust of Cellnet's current advertising theme as well as several BT campaigns in the past.

Organisational capital and politics

Women's capacities to organise, get things done and build institutions are an important aspect of their potential power. In the past, women accumulated a good deal of organisational capital within the community, where they were active in voluntary organisations and in less formal ways. Much of their power was exercised through traditional women's organisations such as the Townswomen's Guild, Women's Institutes and the Mothers' Union. Many women are still active in community action groups and volunteer organisations as well as other local networks. Women are often active as parent governors, sit on community health councils, and on the boards of local quangos. But many of the traditional large scale women's organisations are in decline and face a haemorrhaging of support, partly because so many more women are now in the labour market.[50]

On the other hand, women's organisational capital is being channelled in new ways into the economy, through what has been described as 'business feminism'.[51] Increasing numbers in each new generation are creating their own businesses. For example, while 75 per cent of female students surveyed by *Cosmopolitan* said that they were ambitious, only 38 per cent described themselves as feminist,[52] one symptom of changing perspectives. Over 50 per cent of women who start up their own business do so in order to be their own boss and increase their independence, whereas only 15 per cent are motivated primarily by financial considerations.[53] At the same time women's professional networks are thriving.

Party politics is another outlet for organisational skills. In 1993, one quarter of all councillors in Great Britain were female compared with only 17 per cent in 1976. At the national level the 1992 general election saw the election of 60 women MPs, nearly one in ten, compared with less than 4 per cent in 1983.[54] The introduction of quotas within the Labour party means that the issue of female representation has been firmly put on the agenda;

almost one third of Labour Party MPs will be women after the 1997 general election, and this policy has already put the issue of female representation firmly onto the agenda of the Conservative Party.

But while the machinery of politics is slowly absorbing the women who want to get actively involved, it still has little attraction for the vast majority. A recent survey found that over a third of women were not very interested in politics while only 7 per cent were very interested. Young women in particular are the least likely to be interested in party politics. Only 3 per cent of women are members of a political party.[55] The under-representation of women in politics may account for the failure of parties to address gender issues and the failure of these issues to carry electoral weight. This in turn helps to explain women's increasing disaffection with politics.[56] One response to the failure of the parties to address women's needs has been for women to organise outside the mainstream political arena. Women aged between 18 and 34 are almost five times as likely to be active on the environment as on other issues.[57]

However women have considerable potential electoral power. The Fawcett Society's research on women's voting patterns shows that women vote in larger numbers than men. They are also the majority of floating voters, especially in the key marginal constituencies.[58] As yet, however, and in stark contrast to other countries such as the USA, women's organisations do not appear to have successfully mobilised to ensure that women's priorities and concerns are addressed.

Politics as an external force
Looking ahead there is no shortage of political issues that will acutely affect women. They include fiscal pressures on the welfare state, pressures to use women to provide unpaid long term care, problems of pensions, parental leave and childcare. Because women live longer, and because they are more likely to be taking the lead in childcare, these issues are particularly pressing for them.

Values: no turning back but no clear way forward?

The Demos report *No turning back: generations and the genderquake* demonstrated that feminine values are moving to the core of British society, displacing male values.[59] The core values for Britons as a whole include community and the environment.

As shown on the following maps, the closer two values are, the more likely they are to be held by the same people. Broadly speaking we can map either individuals or groups onto this chart. In the top left hand corner are the more traditional values. The people who are attached to these values are resisting many contemporary trends. In the bottom left hand corner are the people generally satisfied with things, and who are enjoying life. They are more outward going and consumerist. The leading edge values tend to come from the bottom right hand corner,

Dynamics of social change

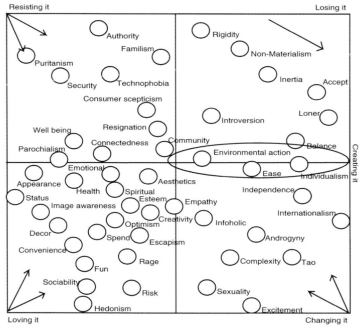

Source: *Insight '96*, Synergy Brand Values Ltd, London, 1997.

and are the values which are changing society. Those in the top right are held by people losing out in life, turning inwards to loneliness and inertia. In general, younger people's values tend to fall more on the bottom right hand side of this chart, with more and more women enjoying life and being strongly attached to the values which are changing society and creating it anew.

Looking ahead, in a linear forecast we would expect the values in the top left hand corner to move further out, those in the bottom right hand corner to move more towards the centre. With continuing peace and prosperity, the 'new core' of values, including ease,

Female genderquakers: 55 per cent of all women, 1996

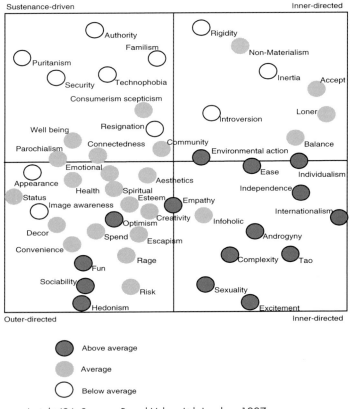

Source: *Insight '96*, Synergy Brand Values Ltd, London, 1997.

individualism, balance and the environment would move into the centre.

This would also imply a continuing change in women's values. Older feminine values are being subtly transformed with the rise of a generation more familiar with complexity and multiple roles; younger women are more at ease with risk, excitement and blurred gender roles.

We can see the effects of this genderquake in the strong attachment to these newer values among the 55 per cent of women who strongly disagree with the statement, 'a man's place is at work, a woman's place is in the home'. These women are more likely to be under 35, and least likely to be over 65.

The extent of the generation gap among women is now well established. It presages further tensions between women, and in reviewing both the Synergy data and the new ten year research comparisons through the *Changing lives* study, we can see signs that women's values and attitudes will fragment still further, making it harder for them to feel solidarity towards each other. Some of the newer values are likely to be disturbing for the mainstream. Examples include women's attachment to hedonism, as manifest in nights out and drugs use, or the greater ease with open discussion of sex, or the attachment of a small minority to violence.[60]

New psychotherapeutic models shed light?

How should we understand women's experiences, and what do they imply for the future? Psychotherapy provides a helpful way in, since it shows that it is perfectly healthy for an individual to consist of multiple sub-personalities, which emerge in different situations and express aspects of self despite the roles that women have in their daily lives. This idea is now widely accepted and used in advertising. Ogilvy and Mather's 1995 study *Releasing the woman within* [61] hypothesised that there is a 'real woman' or 'hedonist' within all women for advertisers to appeal to, although the *Socioconsult* research shows that this is more repressed in older age groups.[62]

Greater freedom to control reproduction and the terms of family life have made it easier for women to develop a mosaic of multiple roles which the diagram opposite identifies.

If we take each of these areas in turn, it is possible to demonstrate from the *Changing lives* data and through data provided by Synergy how different segments have diverged over the last ten years.

Self-identity

Women's self-identity is no longer primarily derived from their role as mothers. Instead, it derives from all sources – from beliefs to jobs. In one survey, 96 per cent of individuals said that being appreciated as an individual was important to them, compared to only 30 per cent who cited having a man in their lives, and only 20 per cent who cited getting married. Eighty-six per cent of women said that they did not think the term housewife described them at all.[63] For many women, particularly singles as the table opposite shows, health and appearance are important sources of self-identity, as are sexuality and freedom.

Family relationships

Although the majority of households no longer conform to the nuclear family model, most women still put the family high on their list of priorities. An overall decline since the mid-1980s masks substantial differences between various groups, with a slight increase in concern for the family among women with children – an indicator of social anxieties about how children are being brought up. But while women with children are the most likely to be concerned with family duty, full-time working women have shown the biggest drop since 1986.

Consumption patterns

Women's behaviour as consumers shows interesting variations. The idea that women will be the driving force for greater corporate responsibility is confirmed as the

The new mosaic of women's choices

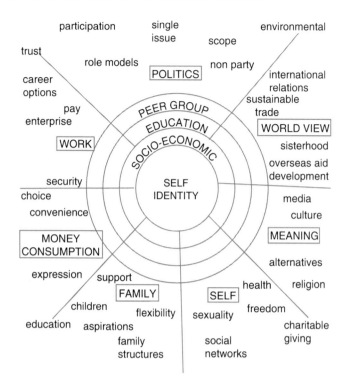

The single woman is more concerned with personal issues

% agreeing that these things concern them	Average 1996	Single women 1996
Buying clothes that express my personality	13	20
Being a creative person	20	24
Staying fit and healthy	71	78

Source: *Changing lives 1996*, AGB Taylor Nelson/Future Foundation, London.

Family duty is still important

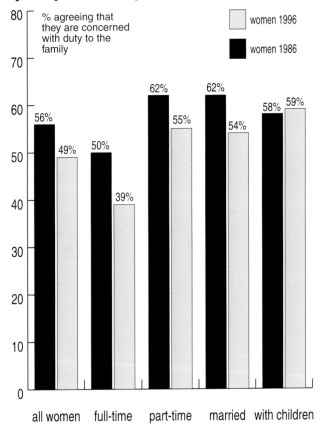

% agreeing that they are concerned with duty to the family

women 1996

women 1986

category	1986	1996
all women	56%	49%
full-time	50%	39%
part-time	62%	55%
married	62%	54%
with children	58%	59%

Source: *Changing lives 1986-1996*, AGB Taylor Nelson/Future Foundation, London.

chart opposite shows, although again, there are substantial differences. Cynicism about company behaviour has increased across the board but that the most significant increase has been among full-time working women. The women with most experience of companies – full time workers – have become the most cynical about company behaviour, perhaps because of the wide gulf between corporate rhetoric and behaviour during the recession of the early 1990s when many were laid off, and companies failed to deliver on their promises for women's opportunities.

Working experience
Job insecurity has grown substantially, particularly affecting women in full-time jobs and single women – not surprisingly perhaps since they are more dependent on a reliable income. These levels of insecurity have changed surprisingly little during a period of falling unemployment (see chart overleaf). Indeed, insecurity could be becoming a permanent part of the working environment, making women more concerned to insure against unemployment, for example through qualifications.

Cynicism is on the increase

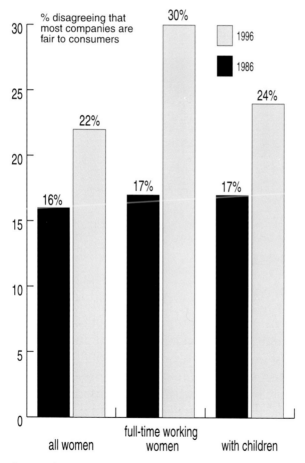

Source: *Changing lives 1986-1996*, AGB Taylor Nelson/Future Foundation, London.

Increasing job insecurity for working and single women

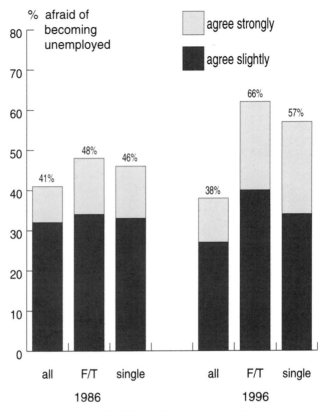

Source: *Changing lives 1986-1996*, AGB Taylor Nelson/Future Foundation, London.

Political values

Patterns of political support reflect the wider story of fragmentation. Support for Labour and the Conservatives among men is roughly constant in all age groups. By contrast, among women there is a massive skew with young women overwhelmingly supporting Labour. Older women are far more likely to vote Conservative, reflecting women's traditional skew to the right.

There are other points of divergence. For working women, even Conservative voters, the minimum wage and low pay are key issues. Lifestage is also critical. For mothers, child benefit is a key issue, while for women over 55 pension provision and buses are particularly important.[64]

World view
Changing lives found that full-time working women are more likely to be concerned with global competition and less concerned about the UK's loss of moral leadership in the world. Non-working women are more likely to blame immigrants for high unemployment than other groups, and women without jobs in lower socioeconomic groups tend to be more focused on the local environment than others. Overall there has been a decline of interest in local

Which parties women vote for

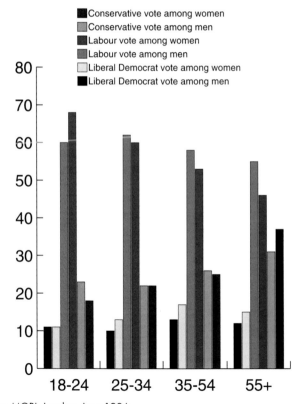

Source: MORI, London, June 1996.

Women's self-identity, 1996

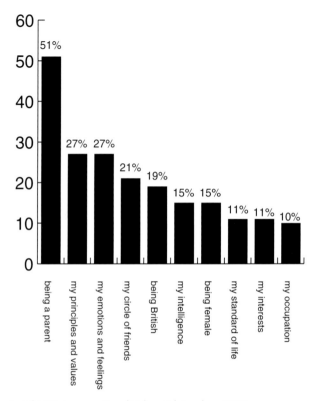

Source: *Insight '96*, Synergy Brand Values Ltd, London, 1977.

issues and community – down by 7 per cent over the decade, although the decline has been less marked for women who are not working.

Beliefs and meaning
There is a growing trend towards the new 'pot pourri' of beliefs and values – combining the more arcane with the mainstream (such as astrology). While the traditional religions have continued to lose adherents, the numbers involved in evangelical, charismatic and new age religions have grown. These seem better able to supply a framework of meaning and belonging than the major religions.

Is there anything called a 'typical woman'

It is hard to define anything approaching a typical woman. Synergy's survey revealed that only 15 per cent of women define themselves by their gender (and these women tend to be single). The majority of women – some 51 per cent – say that their self-identity comes from being a parent. Meanwhile, principles and values, emotions and feelings, circles of friends and being British are considered more important than being a woman per se. Perhaps most striking of all, slightly more women define themselves through their intelligence than through their experience of being a woman. Only standard of living, interests and occupation rank lower.

In some respects, this confirms the progress that has been made. Women no longer need to unite to achieve basic recognition of their rights to vote or to work. There are still some shared issues, such as pay, where the differences between men and women are greater than in any other major European country. But on most issues class, background, generation, culture, values and beliefs are likely to matter more.

The increasing fragmentation of women's lives and interests presents a challenge to politicians and businesses trying to reach out to women. But it also raises the more fundamental question of whether women will ever be able to pull together effectively – whether female solidarity will mean anything in the future.

What does this mean for the way women organise and for the future of feminism? As we have seen, many traditional women's organisations have lost members, many campaigning feminist organisations no longer coalesce into a clearly identifiable movement, and the newer organisations – in business and the professions – tend to be more oriented to careers, networking and individual achievement than politics and collective action. These reflect the kind of 'power feminism' that Naomi Wolf promoted in her book, *Fire with fire*,[65] but their audience remains a small one, and their arguments are only relevant to a minority of women.

Should we conclude that feminism is no longer needed, and will no longer play a part in women's lives in 2010? Certainly, feminism has lost some of its pull. According to survey evidence, although feminist values are widely held, and women are generally positive about feminism and its achievements,[66] few women see themselves as feminist, partly because feminism has been caricatured as unrealistic and extreme but also because it has not paid sufficient attention to family concerns and motherhood.[67]

The 'depoliticisation' of women's issues has been encapsulated in the label 'post-feminism' which is widely used and little defined. Feminism's loss of clarity means that it has failed to deliver in important ways. Although highly influential in culture and philosophy, there has been little influence on practical policy or in terms of thinking about how government should operate. Campaigns to increase numbers of women in business and Parliament have been easier to organise than campaigns to change the ways in which such organisations operate. Although the next parliament will have substantially more women, it is less clear how much their presence will change the shape of the political agenda. The slogan 'the personal is political' helped to shift perceptions of what is important. But as Suzanne Moore says in the introduction to her book *Head over heels*, 'The personal may be political, but if we concentrate purely on the personal we lose sight of the wider picture'.[68] The most newsworthy promise that Labour Shadow Minister for Women Janet Anderson could make about how women's lives might change under a Labour administration was the suggestion that there would be more promiscuity.

Looking ahead, many factors may further transform feminism. While our culture is moving strongly towards greater androgyny, emphasising just how interchangeable male and female identities are, new genetic knowledge could bring a greater awareness of the underlying differences between men and women. One possibility, suggested by Robert Wright in his essay for the *Demos*

Quarterly,[69] is that instead of wanting the law to treat men and women equally, we will again conclude that the law should give additional protections for women as opposed to men, because of awareness that rape and harassment affect women more severely than men. New genetic knowledge will, in this argument, lend added support to the strand of radical feminism which has emphasised the innate differences between men and women.

But the main conclusion to be drawn from the data already set out is that while many of tomorrow's women will probably still be fighting battles for the respect and opportunities that they believe are their due, in most respects they will share less in common than women today. There will be no women's movement, only women's movements; there will be no feminism, only feminisms.

Many will have carried on up a ladder of achievement that would have been unimaginable only a few generations ago, boosted by rising numbers passing through higher education. But for many others life will still be a struggle of hard work, poverty and lack of recognition.

We turn now to our five portraits of tomorrow's women. These portraits – Networking Naomi, New Age Angela, Mannish Mel, Back to Basics Barbara and Frustrated Fran – are inevitably to some extent caricatures.

But they provide a useful lens through which we can think through the opportunities and dilemmas facing millions of British women over the next dozen years. Most women will not identify exactly with any of them, and all women change to some extent as their lives unfold.

But these portraits do have a basis in fact today, in what we know about contemporary values and lives, and it is with these individual women, albeit composite ones, that we now try to unravel the likely patterns of change.

Notes

1. These statistics come from the British household panel study cited in: 'The future is female' in *Planning for social change, 1996-97,* Henley Centre, London, 1996.
2. Figures from the National Office of Statistics. The estimated resident population at mid-1995 (the last year for which figures are available) was 58,605,800, of which 28,727,500 were men and 29,878,300 women.
3. In 1994, average life expectancy for men was 73.9 years, while for women it was 79.2. Central Statistical Office, 1996, *Population trends,* HMSO, London, table 12.
4. In 1971, just over 13 per cent of the United Kingdom population were 65 or over; by the year 2051 this proportion is projected to rise to around 24 per cent. Central Statistical Office, 1995, *Social trends,* HMSO, London, 17.
5. Office of National Statistics, 1997, *Social trends,* HMSO, London.
6. This prediction is drawn from statistics provided by the Office of Population Censuses and Surveys and reported in the *Family Policy Studies Centre Bulletin,* April 1995, Family Policy Studies Centre, London.
7. The average age at which women in the UK marry for the first time rose from 23 years in 1976 to 26 years in 1993, *Pre-family lifestyles,* Mintel, London, 1996, 13.
8. The average age at first birth rose from 25 in 1976 to 29 in 1995, See note 7, 14. The average number of children born per woman has fallen from 3 in 1961 to 1.8 in 1995, *Social focus on women,* Central Statistical Office, London, 1995, 17.
9. See note 5.

10. In the UK over the last four decades there has been a fourfold increase in the number of people cohabiting, Buck N and Scott J, 1994, 'Household and family change' in Buck N, Gershuny J, Rose D and Scott J, eds, 1994, *Changing households: the British household panels survey 1990-1992,* ESRC Research Centre on Micro-Social Change, Colchester. In addition, whereas 65 per cent of women born between 1950-62 who cohabited went on to marry, this is true of only 56 per cent of those born in 1962. Ermisch J, 1995, *Pre-marital cohabitation, child-bearing and the creation of one parent families,* Working paper 95-17, ESRC Research Centre on Micro-Social Change, Colchester.
11.. Wilkinson H and Mulgan G, 1995, *Freedom's children,* Demos, London, 79.
12. See note 5
13. See note 5.
14. The Economist, 1994, *Pocket Britain in figures,* Penguin, London, 180 and also Utting, D, 1995, *Family and parenthood: supporting families, preventing breakdown,* Joseph Rowntree Foundation, York. Mattison K, McAllister F, and Roberts K, 1994, *Divorce today,* Factsheet 4, One Plus One, London. Some 72 per cent of all divorces are initiated by women. Ermisch J, 1993, 'Familia oeconomica: a survey of the economics of the family' in *Scottish Journal of Political Economy,* vol 40 no 4, 357-358. This shows that there is a link between women working and the rate of divorce.
15. Fielding T, 1995, 'Migration and middle class formation in England and Wales 1981-91' in Butler T and Savage M, eds, 1995, *Social change and the middle classes,* UCL Press, London.

16. See note 5.

17. Since 1950, 5 million jobs in the UK have gone from goods producing industries while about 8 million have been created in services, which have tended to be more open to women. Leadbeater C and Mulgan G, 1994, 'The end of unemployment' in *The end of unemployment: bringing work to life*, Demos Quarterly issue 2, Demos, London, 6.

18. The Economist, 1993, *Pocket Britain in figures*, Penguin, London, 83.

19. 'Women work', *The Independent*, 3 December 1996.

20. See note 1 (Henley Centre, 1996).

21. *Review of the economy and employment*, Institute of Economic Research, Warwick, 1994.

22. This is according to Demos' analysis of the British household panel study in 1995. See note 17, 41-42.

23. See note 8 (Central Statistical Office, 1995).

24. In 1995 of students enrolling in undergraduate degree courses, 51 per cent (505,200) were women and 49 per cent (485,100) were men. Fifty-three per cent of female undergraduates received first degrees of either first or upper second class, compared with 46 per cent of men. Figures from press releases PR04 and PR12, Higher Education Statistical Agency, London. A recent study for the Department of Education and Employment among a younger cohort concluded that on the basis of these educational trends, their relative lack of education has almost disappeared as a factor shaping women's relative pay and job opportunities. See also Joshi H and Paci P, 1995, *Wage differentials between men and women*, Department of Employment, 34. This study found that since 1978, the impact of women's education and training deficit on women's wages, known among analysts as the 'attribute gap' has decreased from 9 per cent to just under 0.4 per cent by 1991. In 1997, this gap has indeed reversed as girls now outperform boys.

25. In August 1989 21 companies (11 per cent) of the then Times Top 200 companies had women on their boards. By 1993 the figure was 49 (25 per cent), an increase of 127 per cent. Over the same period the number of women directors increased by over 100 per cent from 24 to 51. Holton V, Rabbetts J and Scrivener S, 1993, *Women on the boards of Britain's top 200 companies: A progress report*, Ashridge Management Research Group, Berkhamstead, 4.

26. Department of Education and Employment, 1996, *Employment and education: key facts on women*, HMSO, London.

27. Central Statistical Office, 1994, *Social trends*, HMSO, London, 59

28. In 1994 the House of Lords ruled that British part time workers must have the same redundancy and unfair dismissal rights as full time workers. The ruling removed provisions of the Employment Protection Act 1978, ruling that the act breached European Union law on equal pay and equal treatment for men and women.

29. Boyer I, 1993, *Flexible working for managers*, Chartered Institute of Management Accountants, London. Review of the book, *Opportunity 2000 Newsletter*, London. Cited in: Wilkinson H, 1994, *No turning back: generation and the genderquake*, Demos, London.

30. *Families and work 1994*, Factsheet 3, International Year of the Family, London.

31. Thomas M, Goddard E and Hunter P, 1994, *General household survey 1992*, OPCS, London.

32. Brannen J, Meszaros G, Moss P and Poland G, 1994, *Employment and family life: a revew of research in the UK (1980-1994)*, Research series no 41, Department of Employment, London, 18.

33. See note 32.

34. See note 24 (Joshi and Paci, 1995).

35. Harkness S and Machin S and Waldfogel J, 1995, *Evaluating the pin money hypothesis: the relationship between women's labour market activity, family income and poverty in Britain*, Discussion paper no WSP/108, Welfare State Programme, London School of Economics, London, 16.

36. For childless couples, women contribute an average of 44 per cent of total household income. See note 1 (Henley Centre, 1996).

37. See note 1.

38. Waldogel J, 1993, *Women working for less: a longitudinal analysis of the family gap*, Discussion paper no WSP/93, Centre for Economic Performance, London School of Economics, London. Women are still on average paid 20 per cent less than men. Opportunity 2000 figures cited in 'Women at work', *The Independent*, 3 December 1996. See also note 24 (Joshi and Paci, 1995). This research shows that women who have been unable to take job protected maternity leave and who have to temporarily exit the workforce are more likely to suffer discrepancies in pay than those who take protected maternity leave and return to work within the time scale.

39. For further detail see Brewster C et al, 1996, *Working time and contract flexibility in the European Union*, Cranfield School of Management, Ashridge.

40. See note 1.

41. In the UK national workforce, women hold 12.3 per cent of all management positions and 3.3 per cent of directorships. Opportunity 2000 figures cited in 'Women at work', *The Independent*, 3 December 1996.

42. See note 39.

43. The poll was carried out in October 1996. 'Is abortion a vote-winner ?', *The Guardian*, 2 January 1997.

44. 'A matter of life', *The Observer*, 5 January 1997.

45. The Future Foundation, 1997, *The new information trade*, Direct Marketing Association, London.

46. See for example, 6 P with Briscoe I, 1996, *On the cards*, Demos, London.

47. The Council of European Professional Informatics Society (CEPIS) is introducing the European Computer Driving Licence (ECDL). This is a basic qualification which indicates that the holder is competent to undertake a series of straightforward tasks using a computer esprit project 22561-ECDL.

48. *Teleculture futures*, The Henley Centre, London, 1996.

49. Alexander M, Burt M, Collinson A, 'Big talk, small talk, BT's strategic use of semiotics in planning its current advertising' in *Journal of the Market Research Society*, vol 37 no 2, 91-102.

50. The National Federation of Women's Institutes' membership has fallen from 467,000 in 1945 to 299,000 in 1992 and members of the

Mothers' Union and the National Union of Townswomen's Guild halved between 1971-1992. Central Statistics Office, 1994, *Social trends 24*, Central Statistical Office, London, 144.

51. For more on this see Wilkinson H, 1996, 'Business feminism' in *The new enterprise culture*, Demos Quarterly issue 8, Demos, London.

52. Siann G and Wilkinson H, 1995, *Gender, feminism and the future*, Demos, London.

53. 'Women in business' in *Barclays Review*, Barclays Bank, London, 1996.

54. See note 3 (Central Statistical Office, 1995), 52.

55. See note 54, 51.

56. Although any comment on women's disaffection with politics must be set within the context of a general increasing disaffection with politics among both men and women, and especially the young. Only 6 per cent of 15 to 34 year olds describe themselves as very interested in politics, according to *Youth and politics*, an unpublished report prepared by the BBC Political Research Unit, outlining the results of a poll conducted by NOP in December and January 1995 and reported on by the BBC.

57. See note 11.

58. Stephenson M, 1996, *Winning women's votes: the gender gap in voting patterns and priorities*, Fawcett Society, London. See also Wilkinson H and Diplock S, 1996, *Soft sell or hard policies: How can the parties best appeal to women?*, Demos, London.

59. Wilkinson H, 1994, *No turning back: generations and the genderquake*, Demos, London.

60. See note 1.

61. *Releasing the woman within*, Ogilvy and Mather, London, 1995.

62. See note 11.

63. *Women on the verge of the millennium*, Grey Advertising, London, 1996.

64. See note 58 (Stephenson, 1996).

65. Wolf N, 1994, *Fire with fire: the new female power and how it will change the 21st century*, Chatto and Windus, London.

66. MORI poll reported on in 'Who's winning the battle of the sexes', *Mail on Sunday*, 25 June 1995.

67. See note 52.

68. Moore S, 1996, *Head over heels*, Viking, London.

69. Wright R, 1996,' The dissent of woman' in *Matters of life and death*, Demos Quarterly, issue 10, Demos, London.

The future is feminine: Networking Naomi

Networking Naomi is one of a new breed of women who have taken advantage of the 'feminising' of business and the professions. She is to be found in some large service organisations, in consulting, the professions and the media. She is active in promoting female networks, particularly at work, and she does what she can to advance feminine values, which she sees as radically different to the masculine values of traditional, hierarchical business. When women take control, she believes, they bring empathy, emotion, care, flatter hierarchies, less hang-ups about status, and their values better fit the sorts of industry that are likely to prosper in the next century. For her, the future is not just female, but also feminine.

Women like Naomi have a strong sense of connectedness. They are not afraid to express emotions, and are spiritual, creative and environmentally conscious. Empathy is a key value and empathy for others is matched by confidence, optimism and a strong sense of self-esteem, helped by a good education, probably a university degree.[1]

Naomi is something of an infoholic, an avid reader of newspapers and magazines and, increasingly, a user of the Internet. She is at ease with flexible gender roles,

Networking Naomi

Networking Naomi's values, 1996

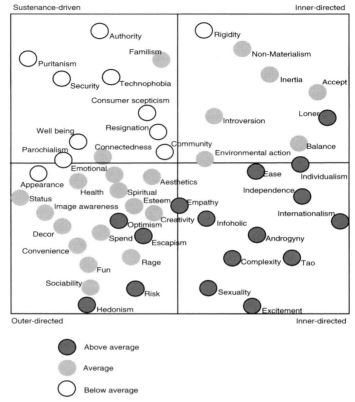

Source: *Insight '96*, Synergy Brand Values Ltd, London, 1997.

having the qualities of a gender chameleon,[2] and is able to dance between masculine and feminine styles of management. She thrives in a fast changing, increasingly complex world and is at ease with it, deriving excitement and a sense of fulfilment from the daily challenges around her. But most important of all, Naomi's sense of purpose and her inner confidence comes from her sense of balance, an ease with herself and her environment, and a willingness to go with the flow which often combines with a strong business acumen.

Women like Naomi see emotions as part of the future not the past: 36 per cent of all women say that most important decisions in their life are based on their emotions, and younger women place a high value on intuition.

Leading examples of this new breed would include Eva Pascoe, founder of the Cyberia cafes; the actress Emma Thompson; the designer and restauranteur Nicole Farhi; and dietician and fitness expert Rosemary Conley. Perhaps the best known example of all would be Anita Roddick who balances business success with a feminine touch as well as deliberately harnessing women's concerns about the environment, rain forests and natural products.

Synergy's research suggests that self-employed women in the 1990s combine these feminine values with a willingness to take risks and greater sociability (both vital for securing new business). Perhaps as a result, they have more self-esteem and optimism than other working women. In the future more of the Networking Naomis will be self-employed.

Who are these women? Generally they are in their twenties, and better educated. Of the 40 per cent of Synergy's sample who are optimistic, the majority are professionals under 35. The 31 per cent who believe in flexible gender roles are also more creative, empathetic, more 'Tao' in their philosophy and also increasingly independent as well as individualistic. In total, about 13 per cent of the women in Synergy's survey fit this picture, combining individualism, empathy, androgyny, optimism and ease with complexity. Looking ahead, there are signs that the numbers of women in this group will grow – partly as a younger generation grows up, partly because the business needs of a service and information based economy will increase the value of communicative skills and empathy, rather than the ability to know your place in a rigid hierarchy, and partly because an ageing society will place ever more emphasis on the values of care. Indeed, if management guru Tom Peters is to be believed, men who wish to stay employed in the future will need to study women's leadership style.

This is perhaps the key. Networking Naomi does not see herself as a response to new challenges and opportunities. Rather she believes that she is the carrier of values which will soon be mainstream for society as a whole.

Women succeeding in the new economy of networks and cooperation in 2010

The feminisation of the economy in terms of the proportion of women in the workforce is set to continue, as the chart below shows.

As we have seen, more women are entering the professions. Eighty per cent of the new jobs forecast to be created by 2000 are expected to go to women.[3] But it is the shift in the nature of the jobs on offer which is promoting feminisation in a qualitative sense. The skills needed in a post-industrial workplace – flexibility, efficiency and good service – are more often associated with women than men and qualities traditionally associated with women – service, dexterity, adaptability, interpersonal skills and perhaps as important in the long run, EQ (emotional intelligence) – are now seen as critical for business success in the future.

In terms of their ability to manage their time, to understand other people's problems, to give good service to customers and to adapt to changing methods of

Economic activity rates by gender and age

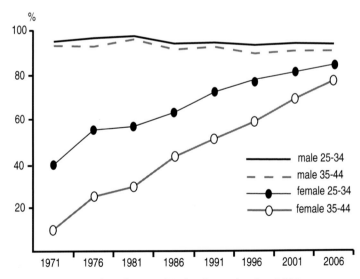

Source: Department of Employment/Henley Centre, London, 1996.

working, both men and women judge women to be better equipped for this new world of work. The only positive characteristic where women lack this lead is the ability to organise others. Men still think they are better at this.

Part of the reason is that, historically, women have had more experience of working in more flexible, cooperative and less secure ways. But as the chart overleaf shows, these approaches to work are also more appealing to women than men precisely because such work offers them flexibility and the chance to spend time with the family. Indeed, part-time work, contract work and home working can all facilitate the balance Naomi seeks in her life.

By 2010, most big firms will probably employ fewer people. One study conducted by Cranfield School of Management for the European Union showed that over 40 per cent of firms surveyed in the UK reported an increase

Is the future female?

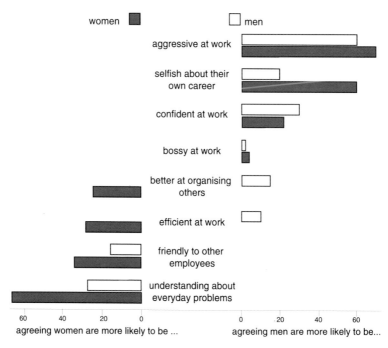

Source: *Planning for social change 1995-96*, The Henley Centre, London.

Why women work part time

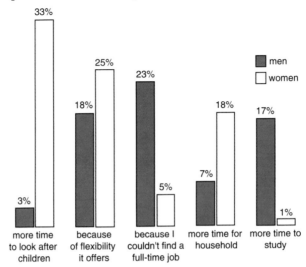

Source: *Planning for social change 1995-96*, Henley Centre, London.

in sub-contracting and an increase in the use of temporary and short term contracts (see chart on next page). Most anticipate further contracting out in the years ahead. More jobs will be temporary, part time, insecure, and more will involve face to face interaction with other employees or with customers.

Unless there is a dramatic shift in male attitudes to work and in society's views of men's skills, by 2010 these changes will have benefited women. Already, men are almost twice as likely as women to experience redundancy.[4]

Readiness for change makes women better prepared for developing new skills throughout their careers. Women have traditionally been more accustomed to discontinuous employment and are therefore better prepared psychologically for having to retrain regularly to remain employable. Gail Sheehy[5] talks of a 'second adulthood' for women who take up new careers and education later in life, and many women are already 'serial careerists'.

Much of the change will take place in management,

The slimmed down corporation

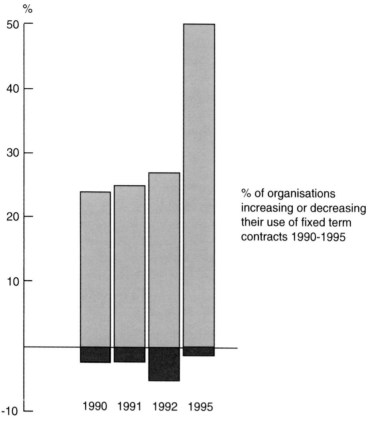

% of organisations increasing or decreasing their use of fixed term contracts 1990-1995

Source: *Working time and contract flexibility in the European Union*, Cranfield School of Management, Ashridge, 1996.

the fastest growing broad jobs category in the 1990s. While in Britain as a whole each new decade is creating roughly 1 million new management jobs (net), many analysts confidently predict that the proportion of these jobs to be filled by women will be substantially higher in 2010 than it is today.[6] If women managers are finally in the majority, the hope is that they will do more to shape corporate cultures to value women employees. According to this view, the typical firm will come to define itself through childcare provision, flexible time arrangements and the absence of formal job titles and rigid tiers of authority. Wage differentials between men and women might even be reversed as female skills become more highly valued. Flexible work combined with a feminine management style could be positively female friendly for *all* working women.

But the biggest changes could come from outside the big organisations. As firms move away from being 'employing' organisations to 'organising' organisations,

The flexible firm

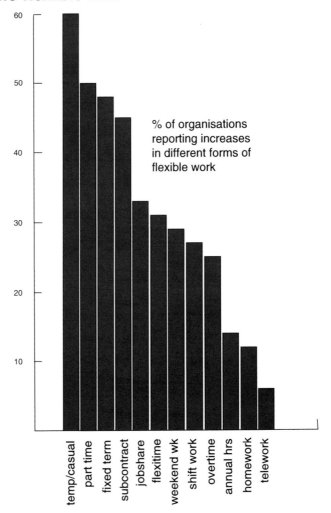

% of organisations reporting increases in different forms of flexible work

Source: *Working time and contract flexibility in the European Union*, Cranfield School of Management, Ashridge, 1996.

with a much reduced core of people managing the firm while operational tasks are sub-contracted to businesses and individuals on the periphery, small and medium sized companies will proliferate. Indeed they will be key features of the service-based economy of the next century. United States trend data already shows that as many as 40 per cent of these small firms are owned and managed by women, and they will thrive in the flatter, shifting, skills based work structures of 2010.[7] Perhaps because of this, when asked how they would advise an 18 year old woman today about her career options, Demos' survey of Forum UK members (the elite professional organisation for women) found that nearly twice as many would recommend a young woman to set up her own business as would recommend working in a large company with a fixed career structure.

As well as providing services for larger companies, many of these will collaborate in new ways described by Charles Savage in *Fifth generation management* as 'value sharing and knowledge networking'.[8]

Precisely because women are more at ease with networks and cooperation which rely on the active nurturing of trust, the telephone will continue to provide the basis for much business interaction in 2010. It is no accident that BT's boss in their advertisements encouraging small firms to use new technology is a woman. Telephones will maintain the 'human touch' in women's networks, building trust and empathy to counter the anonymity of other electronic forms of information exchange.

We also anticipate that younger women will increasingly be undertaking more complex forms of information exchange as they shape the Internet to their own needs. Although there is a technology gap among women as a whole, there is little discrepancy between younger professional men and women in terms of their technological literacy, and many of the leading entrepreneurs in the industries rising up around the Net and multimedia are women.

This new networking culture will create a ready demand for new technologies. Increasingly sophisticated 'intelligent agents' – which can seek out personalised information and contacts, or cheaper prices – will have lured women on to the Net in numbers more closely matching men's. Innovations ranging from screened e-mail and newsgroup activity through to software which recognises voices and handwriting could all have made the interface with the Net not only more user-friendly, but more relevant too. They could help to close the gap between more technically literate men and women who are less at ease with text-based systems.[9]

Exercising consumer power to make the world a better place in 2010

Women's experience and sophistication as consumers is an under-used strength in their march towards equality. If women become more powerful and more confident at work, we should also expect them to become more confident about using their power as consumers to change corporate behaviour. Women's anger at 'immoral' company behaviour has remained consistently high, as the chart on the next page shows. Full-time working women and those with children show the biggest increases in this ten year period.

Women tend to be in the lead in ethical consumerism and ethical investing. Forty-one per cent of British consumers are now, at least in a weak sense, 'green consumers' and precisely because women still spend more time on cooking and shopping than men, they are able to use their power pro-actively in terms of the products they buy.[10] From 1990 to 1996 there was a 140 per cent increase in the amount of 'green produce' purchased.[11] Purchases of 'fair trade' products such as Cafe Direct and Clipper Tea have steadily risen. Pressure groups such as Women for Women – which supports the implementation of International Labour Organisation standards for homeworkers with the slogan 'the labour behind the label' – are on the rise. Companies like The Gap and Levi Strauss

Anger at unethical business remains high

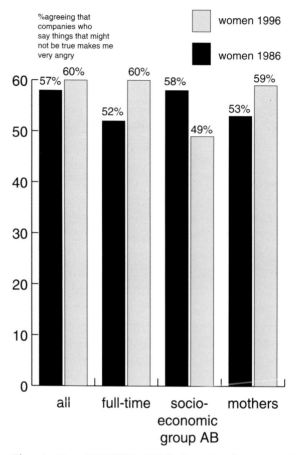

%agreeing that companies who say things that might not be true makes me very angry

women 1996

women 1986

Source: *Changing Lives 1986-1996*, AGB Taylor Nelson/Future Foundation, London.

(notable for their younger clientele) have well-developed policies on labour and social standards and Sainsbury's has committed itself to ethical branding of their own products by 1998. Marks and Spencers and Burton also have guidelines on labelling and sourcing products. In the USA, child labour campaigns and boycotts caught the attention of President Clinton, who took the issue seriously. Alongside the rise of ethical investment – up nearly tenfold in the last decade – the net effect is a cultural shift in how people think about their role in the market, a shift from passive to active engagement.

Women's rising confidence could also change the shape of markets, weakening the current distribution and retailing networks which are dominated by large branded retailers. Given their greater time pressures, women are likely to be in the forefront of ordering groceries direct from home – via electronic methods using the telephone or digital television. They are already far more experienced as home shoppers than men: some 25 per cent (generally in lower socio-economic groups) have acted as agents and over 45 per cent have purchased in this way compared to 25 per cent of men.[12]

If the future really is feminine we should expect more local, personalised, and cooperative distribution services geared to delivering convenience – such as home laundry delivery services – and these in turn will help to create local, flexible employment opportunities.

New models of consumption could also feed back in other ways into opportunities for women at work. If, in marketing and communications, consumer values replace a 'masculine' model of control and campaigns with a more 'feminine' model of openness, interaction and listening, women should be the main beneficiaries.

Flexible, supportive, non-traditional families predominate

For women to dominate the work environment, they will have to be supported in their roles as mothers and partners. While two-thirds of parents with dependent children are both working, there are only about 600 workplace nurseries available.[13] Unlike other countries in northern Europe, we have no state scheme of parental leave and few employer leave schemes.[14] A more confident female workforce could successfully demand concessions, both from employers and from government. But they may also be able to develop alternative solutions, with greater use of homework and telecommuting. New support and childcare networks, like the Parents Network and Home Start schemes, could also play a role.

More women adopt a balanced approach

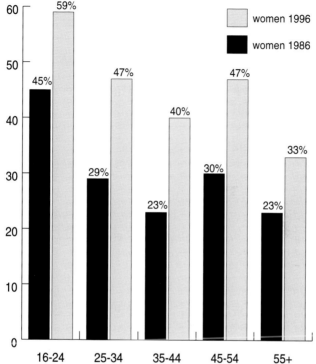

% agreeing they
get equal satisfaction
from home and work

Legend:
- women 1996
- women 1986

Age group	women 1986	women 1996
16-24	45%	59%
25-34	29%	47%
35-44	23%	40%
45-54	30%	47%
55+	23%	33%

Source: *Changing lives 1986-1996*, AGB Taylor Nelson/Future Foundation, London.

At home, Networking Naomi will be changing the ethos of parental involvement. For her, motherhood is neither a necessity nor an unwelcome chore. It is a richly meaningful experience – perhaps more than any other – and one she wants to get the most out of. This means not only attending more parenting classes, but also ensuring there is time to spend with the children.

Fitter and fulfilled

Naomi will be concerned to spend time and energy on her fitness and health. *Changing lives* data suggests that fitness and health will remain at the top of the agenda for economically empowered working women – as it was already in 1986. With economic prospects secured by changes in the workplace, women will veer even more strongly towards self-fulfilment as their main overall goal. The *Changing lives* data shows that younger women (16 to 24 year olds) remain significantly more concerned with achieving balance: the proportion rose from 45 per cent in 1986 to 59 per cent in 1996 (see chart overleaf).

Feminised politics and women's world view

Despite a female prime minister, British politics is almost the last place to show signs of the future being feminine. Even by the time of the election after next, the proportion of MPs who are women will still be under 15 per cent. But other countries have shown that it is possible to achieve a rapid 'feminisation' of politics. Many Scandinavian countries have rough parity between men and women,[15] and at one point Iceland had a female president, speaker of the house and head of the judiciary. Here, the Labour Party has tried to sharply increase its numbers of women MPs with some success. The effect of a likely doubling in their complement of women MPs could put pressure on the other parties – as happened in Norway where the Labour Party opted in the early 1980s for a 40 per cent quota of female candidates, quickly forcing a response from the other parties. Once a critical mass has been achieved,[16] it is likely that a new generation of MPs will reform parliament's working practices to better reflect women's needs, bringing to an end its extraordinarily anachronistic ways of working. With shorter working hours and online voting systems, the shooting range will have been converted into a creche and the smoky bars of the House transformed into family friendly cafes.

The networking spirit could also change the way politics is done, with widespread video-conferences within the parliamentary parties, and for select committees and parliamentary debates, so that women MPs can address the house from the comfort of their living room.

In the United States, women's political power is now well entrenched, following campaigns on abortion and sexual harassment which contributed to big increases in the numbers of pro-choice and pro-feminist governors, senators and representatives (male and female) in the early 1990s.[17] Under President Clinton, the cult of the femocrat (a phrase first coined in Australia), meaning the female bureaucrat, has taken hold, as a new caste of female politicians and administrators have learned to wield power.

For believers in a feminine future, other changes should also follow. Consensus should push out conflict, alongside electoral systems that promote inter-party cooperation rather than polarisation. The success of the Women's Coalition in Northern Ireland in achieving incremental change through compromise and good humour is just one example of the way in which feminine values of cooperation and consensus building can be a source of energy, optimism and rejuvenation even in a region gridlocked in its politics.[18] For the optimists, the result of feminisation would be a revival of trust in political institutions (public confidence in parliament is now down to 10 per cent),[19] while the monarchy might remodel itself in a feminine style, taking forward the legacy of the Queen Mother and the Queen into a Scandinavian style monarchy – under Queen Anne, or perhaps even Princess Di, 'queen of hearts', chosen in preference to Charles in a referendum in 2003.

Fertility

The final plank in the vision of a feminine future comes from biology. If male fertility continues to decline,[20] what will this do to the balance between men and women? Will the remaining fertile males be used to provide sperm to a large number of women? Perhaps artificial insemination by donor will become the norm by the early decades of the next century.

Naomi's uncertain futures

The big uncertainty about the world view promoted by
Networking Naomi is what happens to men. How will
they respond? Will they welcome the chance to discover
the feminine side of their character? Or will they react
like most groups losing power – with resentment and
anger? If they do act defensively to protect their powers
then the benign outlook of women like Naomi will be less
sustainable. Instead we should expect conflict, with men
battling for special treatment in schools and in the jobs
market, and with women becoming more assertive in
response.

The other great uncertainty is whether the equation
between the presence of women and the presence of
feminine values is really credible. Many would argue that,
as women become more powerful, gender differences in
values will become less apparent. Women will
increasingly give up their nurturing qualities, and they
will enjoy the power and prestige that men have so long
monopolised for themselves. There is also a question over
the relative importance of Networking Naomi. Although
her attributes are common among the most successful
younger women, she constitutes only about an eighth of
all women. Even though these numbers look set to
increase, many more women are experiencing an
altogether less rosy life in the workplace and at home.

Signs of the times

femininity	⊙ androgyny
shop 'til you drop	⊙ home delivery
trade fairs	⊙ fair trade
job for wife	⊙ portfolio careers
femininity	⊙ flexibility
professionals	⊙ professionelles
core values	⊙ care values
women's work	⊙ jobs for the girls
everyone for themselves	⊙ lean on me
balance sheet	⊙ inner balance
status	⊙ empathy
corporate ethos	⊙ ethical business
jobs for the boys	⊙ networks for the girls
workaholic	⊙ infoholic
2.4 children	⊙ 1.8 children
pin money	⊙ PEP
business men	⊙ gender chameleons
executive toys	⊙ toys
Dow Index	⊙ Taoism
secretary	⊙ executary
on-the-go	⊙ on-line
IQ	⊙ EQ
cereal providers	⊙ serial careerists
gynaecology	⊙ child psychology
work or family	⊙ work family
the body beautiful	⊙ male anorexia
motherhood	⊙ active parenting
managers	⊙ womanagers
sympathy	⊙ empathy
disconnection	⊙ connexity
human face	⊙ interface
the 7.52 from platform 1	⊙ telecommuting
bureaucrat	⊙ femocrat
feminism	⊙ feminisms
cottage industry	⊙ telecottaging

Notes

1. This demographic profile has been developed through Synergy Brand Values dataset. See appendix.

2. 'It's a macho man's world', *Independent on Sunday*, 9 February 1997.

3. More than half of new solicitors are women (there are already more female solicitors under 30 than male ones), and girls are now outperforming boys in schools in both the arts and sciences.central Statistical Office, 1995, *Social focus on women*, HMSO, London, 8.

4. Brewster C et al, 1996, *Working time and contract flexibility in the European Union*, Cranfield School of Management, Ashridge.

5. Sheehy G, 1996, *New Passages*, HarperCollins, London.

6. Cannon and Taylor Working Party Report, 1994, *Management development to the millenium*, Institute of Management, Corby.

7. Wilkinson H, 1996,'Business feminism' in *The new enterprise culture*, Demos Quarterly issue 8, Demos, London, 13.

8. Savage C, 1996, *Fifth generation management*, Butterworth-Heinemann, Massachussetts.

9. Pescovitz D and Wieners B, 1996, *Reality check*, Hardwired Books, San Francisco.

10. Thirteen per cent of the average weekly expenditure of households is on food, more than for any other single category, including housing according to figures cited in the ONS Family Expenditure Survey, cited in NOP, 1997, *The financial marketing pocket book*, NTC Publications Ltd, London.

11. This data is taken from a paper presented by Bob Worcester, Chairman of MORI to the Centre for the Study of Environmental Change, Lancaster, 27 September 1996.

12. BMRB, 1994, *Target Group Index*, Synergy Brand Values, London.

13. *Childcare now*, Briefing paper 1, Daycare Trust, London, 1997.

14. See Wilkinson H and Briscoe I with Martin Kaye, 1996, *Parental leave – the price of family values?*, Demos, London. Demos will be publishing the results of an extensive survey of the availability of parental leave among employers.

15. See Lovenduski J, 'Will quotas make Labour more women-friendly?' in *Renewal*, vol 1, January 1994.

16. See for example, Castle S, 'The Cabinet of tomorrow?', *Independent on Sunday*, 9 February 1997. This article predicts that 1997 will be a year of opportunity for the new political generation.

17. Wolf N, 1993, *Fire with fire: the new female power and how it will change the 21st century*, Chatto and Windus, London, 6-7.

18. 'All together now', *The Guardian*, 17 February 1997.

19. *Planning for social change, 1996-97*, Henley Centre, London, 1997.

20. A study by Finnish scientists published in the *British Medical Journal* revealed a drop in numbers of men capable of normal sperm production – from 56.4 to 26.9 per cent – between 1981 and 1991. 'A matter of life...', *The Observer*, 5 January 1997. Another study found that there was a fall of 20 per cent in the average sperm count among men born after 1971, in comparison with those born before 1959. The study was carried out by Stewart Irvine of the Medical Research Council. 'Science and sperm', *The Guardian*, 9 March 1996.

Postmaterial-ism beckons: New Age Angela

Angela has the status and wealth to match men. But she doesn't find conventional success and the accumulation of material wealth a satisfying way to live. Because women have historically been excluded from generating and owning much of the nation's wealth, women like Angela are still relatively rare, but their numbers are growing. As women have made inroads into business, politics, the media, medicine and industry, many have rejected the lifestyle that success on male terms brings with it. Too much time at the office means not enough with the children, or pursuing other interests. It leaves no space for being creative, spiritual, or engaged in the local community. Angela believes that there is more to life and that life should be a *personal* voyage of discovery. Conventional definitions of success are simply too narrow to have much meaning.

According to Synergy's evidence postmaterial woman is to be found across the class and age range, although she is least numerous among women over 65. If she is in work, she is likely to have already achieved success, to have a family and to feel that she can develop herself in other ways.

Today, only a fairly small minority – some 14 per cent –

New Age Angela

of women hold Angela's values. Combining an invidualistic ethos with empathy, she is optimistic, full of self esteem and seeking spiritual fulfilment. Angela is one of the 26 per cent of women in Synergy's sample who believe that they are 'part of a world consciousness or spirit'. She is also concerned about the environment and is prepared to do without things to this end. 60 per cent of all women in Synergy's sample say that they would stop buying a product if they knew it was harming the environment and 78 per cent say that there are many things they could do without.

Seeking to simplify her life, Angela has less need of convenience products than other women. Neither status-

New Age Angela's values, 1996

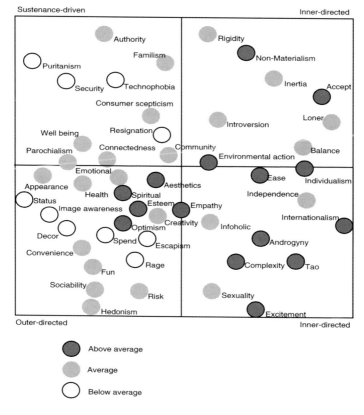

Source: *Insight '96*, Synergy Brand Values Ltd, London, 1977.

oriented nor image-aware, she is less concerned about possessions and home decor (although she is an aesthete and has an eye for the beauty of things for its own sake). No doubt her creativity is put to good use making the best of simple things or products in the home. A minimalist at heart, given her environmental concerns, her house is likely to be spacious, with large spartan white walls, tall exotic plants and natural wood products. Less angry or frustrated than other women, she is nevertheless not particularly sociable. She is neither escapist nor a hedonistic pleasure seeker. A colour therapist would tell Angela that she has a blue aura – calm, and unflappable.

She often feels that she is swimming against the dominant tide. Yet in spite of this, she is nevertheless accepting of others, and relatively at ease with the world around her. Synergy's research suggests that women like her are strongly attached to the 'Tao' value also accept life as it is, 'go with the flow' and have a fluid view of life. She combines an international awareness with a distinctly personal world view, directing her energies inwards rather than into changing the world around her. The only political issue which really galvanises her is the environment.

There are many well-known examples of new age women, ranging from Lynne Franks, Bel Mooney, Linda McCartney and Goldie Hawn to younger examples like Sophie Grigson, Sonja Nuttall and Neneh Cherry. New age values have become widespread over the last two decades, entering the mainstream through alternative medicine and food, environmentalism and culture.

Some of the best examples have rejected careers. For several decades the media have been fascinated by high profile defectors from the career ladder, such as Penny Hughes, the 34 year old female chief executive of Coca Cola UK or Maeve Haran who left a top job at London Weekend Television and started a second, more flexible career as a blockbuster novelist (her first book was called appropriately *Having it all*). Other high flying corporate women such as Linda Kelsey (former editor of *She*) and

Women's concern about the environment is on the increase

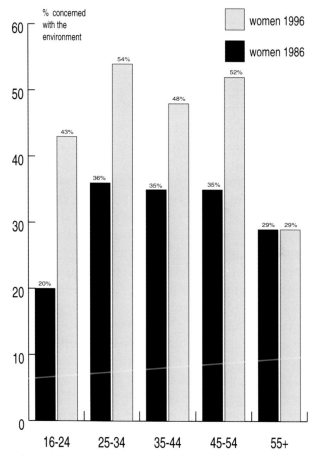

Source: *Changing lives 1986-1996*, AGB Taylor Nelson/Future Foundation, London.

Marcelle D'Argy Smith (former editor of *Cosmopolitan*) have all extolled the pleasures of leaving the rat race.

If superwoman provided a dominant image of womanhood in the 1980s, a more balanced model may be taking over in the late 1990s. Even Madonna, the ultimate 'material girl' of the 1980s who would stop at nothing to get attention has self-consciously reinvented herself in the 1990s, delighting in motherhood and quality time. At a recent awards ceremony she said that she had almost decided not to attend because she couldn't bear to leave her baby.[1] Hollywood actresses – including Michelle Pfeiffer and Demi Moore – now structure their projects to leave them time to spend with their growing broods of children.

All of these women enjoy the benefits of having already made it, with the material wealth to support a more balanced lifestyle. But as a role model such a way of living is proving attractive to younger women with higher educational attainments[2] and more experience of travel and of cultures other than those of the consumerist West.[3]

Today, only a fairly small minority of women hold Angela's values. But there are signs that these numbers are set to grow. Studies of value change show that younger women are more 'postmaterialist' than older generations, and they predict that prosperity tends to make material acquisition less central as a motivation.[4] As the table on the previous page shows, environmental concerns have increased among all age groups of women over the last decade.

The desire for fulfilment also easily outweighs the wish to afford things (36 per cent overall compared to 22 per cent in 1986), and this wish for fulfilment is particularly strong among the younger, full-time working and more affluent segments of the female population.[5]

The world view of women like Angela is amplified by the media, as, for example, in the proliferation of articles about 'downshifting' in the 1990s, many by women writers.[6] Perhaps part of the appeal is that many women would like to be able to achieve a better balance but have neither the courage nor the financial support to do so.

What pushes women in this direction? In some cases a generational experience can be formative, as it was for many women brought up in the 1960s, and in a very different way for the men and women described in Douglas Coupland's *Generation X*.[7] Others may have seen their parents burnt out by overwork, while others still experience a later, mid-life, perhaps post-menopausal, crisis of meaning. Gail Sheehy in her book *New passages*,[8] suggests that women are increasingly developing new interests and identities later in life.

There is also a parallel story involving men. In the past many found their identity through work. But as labour markets have become less secure and as many are having to play a fuller role in parenting, their sources of meaning and identity are becoming more diverse. Bad

The search for fulfilment continues to be more important to the more affluent women

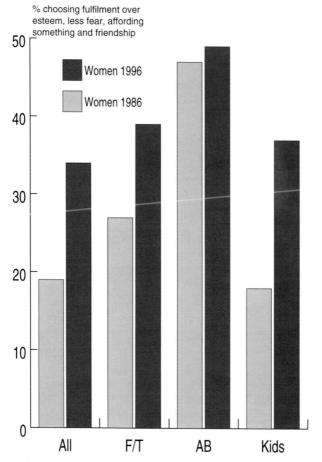

% choosing fulfilment over esteem, less fear, affording something and friendship

■ Women 1996

▫ Women 1986

Source: *Changing lives 1986-1996*, AGB Taylor Nelson/Future Foundation, London.

fortune at work makes people less likely to believe in competitive individualism; but good fortune too can provide the space to pursue less materialist goals.[9] In a recent Henley Centre survey, 62 per cent of men agreed that 'dedicating yourself to your job isn't worth the sacrifices that you have to make'.[10]

In general, postmaterialism is for the well-off. Only a minority of the *Changing lives* sample now opt for insecure employment where their contribution makes a real difference over a secure job where their performance makes no difference to company survival. Full-time working women are no different from their male counterparts in this respect. In spite of their aspiration to more postmaterial values, women as well as men are not yet prepared to take risks to live them out.

In the longer run, however, insecurity could eat away at conventional materialist values. American sociologists have described how the American middle class has moved from contentment to anxiety as big firms have stripped away layers of white-collar jobs.[11] From anxiety it is but a small step to concluding that there is no point in devoting your whole life to an organisation that will happily spit you out when you are no longer needed. For a younger generation who no longer believes that firms can offer

Full-time working women not moving beyond risk yet

If you had to make a choice, which would you pick?	1986	1996
Job security	40%	65%
Insecure but rewarding job	60%	35%

Source: *Changing lives 1996*, AGB Taylor Nelson/Future Foundation, London.

them a job for life, the attractions of achieving a more balanced way of living are obvious.[12] Whereas in the past security came from subsuming yourself within a large organisation, today you may need to take risks to be secure – perhaps starting your own business or becoming self-employed. Then at least you can be in control of your life.

What forces could multiply the numbers of New Age women? One force is likely to be the pressure on time for families and worries about a parenting deficit.[13] Reports of the psychological impact of working mothers on children receive high profile coverage. Less attention has been drawn to the fathering deficit. Nevertheless the latest data on working hours published in *Parenting in the 1990s*[15] shows that more than 25 per cent of fathers are working 50 or more hours per week, an undoubted cause of stress and strain not just on working mothers but also on their children.

Demos' own extensive discussions with young fathers have shown that many want to become more involved in parenting but feel incapacitated either through the pressure of long hours or the lack of father-friendliness in companies.[16] The *Changing lives* data shows that both women and men rank as top priorities the achievement of balance between home and outside sources of satisfaction. If firms cannot deliver balance through more family-friendly employment policies there will be even greater impetus for 'dropping out' of high flying career paths in the future. Opting out or downshifting has in the past been a common option for women but increasingly it has become an option for many men as well.

The second alternative is that if feminine power and feminine values do advance in the way described in the previous chapter, then much of the postmaterial ethos will be absorbed into the mainstream, benefiting not just the high fliers, but also many other women. Rather than being a reaction against the norms of the workplace, the post-material ethos could help to shape those norms instead.

Work – flexibility and freedom are the priority for post-material women

For many, postmaterialism is likely to take the form of a conscious but affordable downshift – a positive choice to pursue fulfilling work, rather than work which is well renumerated. Some will work part time, or from home, or in a looser arrangement with their former employers. Some may be network marketers for good causes – it is already becoming fashionable to sell educational books and organic foods in this way. But the promise of greater freedom may not be realised. Self-employment can be gruelling. A recent survey[17] of freelance translators across the EU found that one in ten were working more than 70 hours a week, 12 per cent were working more than 60 hours a week and 20 per cent at least 50 hours. Much of their work is seen as urgent by the clients and few dare to turn work away. Another study found that while female entrepreneurs clearly have more autonomy than their peers in large scale organisations, the time demands of the business remain a problem for a substantial minority, as do the problems of maintaining a balance between work and family life.[18] Only if they can learn to say no and manage to control their time, will they be able to realise their goals.

The vigilantes of the consumer world?

Women like Angela buy goods that fit in with a postmaterial lifestyle. Aesthetics are important, but so too are the values that products embody. The advent of shops such as the Body Shop and products such as Cafe Direct, fair trade coffee, means that environmental concerns and business ethics have become economic commodities. *Changing lives* data shows that it is particularly richer, full-time working women and those with children, who are likely to want to do what they can to protect the environment.

Angela is likely to be a buyer of organic vegetables, clothing made from natural fibres and holidays to rainforests. As someone who is concerned to save time, she is likely to be an eager user of telephone and online services to order everyday goods and services. Much of her consumption will be active rather than passive. She will tend to prefer to cook rather than to buy ready-packaged meals; she will prefer active rather than passive holidays, reading rather than television.

Her consumption patterns may also have an edge, making her one of the 'vigilante consumers',[19] vigilant to the impact of the products she buys on the environment, or in terms of their healthiness. This will be particularly true of food, where the steadily rising number of scares

The more you have got the less you want

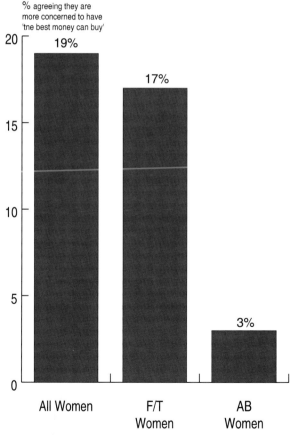

% agreeing they are more concerned to have 'tne best money can buy'

Source: *Changing lives 1996*, AGB Taylor Nelson/Future Foundation, London.

and anxieties shows no signs of diminishing. For her, affluence doesn't translate into extravagance. Synergy's data shows that Angela's confidence in her own values means that she has almost no interest in 'having the best money can buy'. *Changing lives* data confirms this trend with fewer than 5 per cent of AB women expressing concern about having the best that money can buy, five times less than women as a whole (see the chart overleaf).

Family: balance is all

In the late 1990s affluent and professional women are the most dependent on formal childcare arrangements.[20] But in the future, for women like Angela balance will be a key issue in family life. Having already achieved success at work, she may reject delegating childcare to a professional on a full-time basis, partly because she wants to enjoy the experience of parenting for herself, and partly because she knows about the potentially harmful effects of over-dependence on childcare for the child itself.

Technological advances will make it easier for Angela to spend quality time with her children, even if she is still working in some form. She will be keen to take advantage of self-drive vehicles which could free up dead time within the first two decades of the next century, transforming the school run and allowing Angela to spend even more 'quality time' with her children rather than focusing on traffic conditions. By the early 1990s adults were spending 900 million hours each year escorting children to school with the proportion of schoolchildren going to school unaccompanied falling from 70 per cent in 1971 to 7 per cent in 1990.[21]

Angela is likely to be in the vanguard of taking the home 'edutainment' revolution to heart. Nearly three quarters of parents with a PC at home believed that it had helped their children become more creative and 43 per cent said that their children's homework grades had improved as a result of using a computer.[22] Given that the computer could become the centrepiece of the twenty first century sitting room in the way television has dominated the twentieth century, Angela may pioneer a trend to home learning. We expect her to use new technology to overcome geographical boundaries and constraints on parental choice by enrolling her children at their preferred school, and taking in interactive lessons, classroom conferencing and electronically filing homework through the Internet, facilitating the growth of virtual schools and universities. Increasingly worried by large class sizes and concerned about inadequate school security (already evident in the 1990s) Angela may lead a return to educating children at home while at the same time seeking an outlet for her own creativity through virtual degrees and other courses which not only satisfy her desire for intellectual stimulation and self-exploration but also ease her way back into the job market once she is ready for new challenges.

Self-improvement, creativity and health continue to be top concerns

Tomorrow's New Age woman will be a big consumer of all things 'alternative'. She will be an eager user of alternative health and psychotherapeutic treatments for herself and her family, and will be encouraged by the speed with which alternative treatments have become mainstream. She will take retreats, and spend large sums on health clubs and alternative holidays.

She will take comfort from the growing acceptability of new forms of treatment. Princess Diana consults the feminist psychotherapist Susie Orbach, and even the Duchess of York, a model of indulgent consumerism, consulted the mystic counsellor, Madame Vasso. Despite controversies over the effectiveness of the myriad of new methods and treatments she will probably be satisfied with what she gets: recent research by the Consumer's Association indicated high levels of satisfaction among those consulting alternative practitioners.[23]

Meaning and world view: but what about enacting change?

Angela takes her responsibilities to society and the wider world seriously. When women like her do become active they are very good at it – as shown by the success of women protesting against the export of veal calves. But at the moment it is Angela's inner directedness which seems more striking. She is not instinctively interested in politics and the public realm, and tends to see it as inauthentic and irrelevant. There is not much sign of this changing in the near future, since women with this set of values are unlikely to push themselves into a political career. But it is possible that disappointment with private life, with the failures of schools, public transport and the environment, could impel women like Angela into political activism.

Angela's uncertain futures

What then are the uncertainties? The positive reasons for believing that postmaterialism is advancing include the likelihood of economic growth and the clear trends towards a feminising of male values. But there are countervailing forces. One is that women like Angela could generate acute resentment from those less fortunate than themselves. Indeed women who have to struggle to compete in traditional environments where flexible working or parental leave is not available and who have to work long hours just to make ends meet are not likely to be sympathetic. They could become hostile to the sort of environmental and flexi-time agenda that postmaterial women espouse. In a more unequal society, postmaterial values may come to be seen as symptoms of the problem rather than as solutions.

Another factor is that in times of economic recession, many women may simply jettison these more postmaterial values and aspirations. This has certainly happened in the past. Alternatively, growing competitive pressures on countries like the UK and US could squeeze out alternative lifestyles as 'unaffordable', as has happened to some extent since the early 1980s with rising working hours.

More complex outcomes are also possible. Women like Angela could indirectly allow politicians and commentators to point to high profile defections from the world of work as proof that women's place is in the home. In any case there are some areas of common ground between the traditionalists and the postmaterialists that could become politically significant.

Perhaps the biggest question mark concerns the broader shift of societal values. If society as a whole is moving beyond materialism then New Age or postmaterial values will spread through all classes and all age groups, rather as liberal attitudes to personal relationships have over the last twenty years.

But that probably depends on a sense of relative security. The more threatened society feels, whether by economic competitors or by the internal dangers of crime or drugs, the less space there may be for the New Age. Instead of being the harbinger of a new society, it could instead remain a niche – rather like the female spiritualists and theosophists of the late nineteenth century with whom today's New Agers share so much in common.

Signs of the times

rational	⊙ emotional
the age of anxiety	⊙ new age
material wealth	⊙ spiritual health
fabric conditioner	⊙ life's rich fabric
material girl	⊙ maternal girl
women's rights	⊙ animal rights
Greenham Common	⊙ Brightlingsea
breaking through	⊙ walk on by
gender gap	⊙ class gap
security	⊙ satisfaction
rhythm method	⊙ *Persona*
assertiveness training	⊙ neuro-linguistic programming
interior design	⊙ feng shui
down-sizing	⊙ down-shifting
menopause	⊙ second adulthood
material wealth	⊙ cultural capital
parenting deficit	⊙ parental fulfilment
right buy	⊙ buy right
TV dinners	⊙ organic produce
if you've got it, flaunt it	⊙ no colour, no perfume, just kind
cosmetic enhancement	⊙ essential oils
post-modern	⊙ minimalist
swimming against the tide	⊙ swimming with dolphins
7 nights in Benidorm	⊙ 3 months in Brazil
the school run	⊙ home edutainment
the F-plan diet	⊙ colonic irrigation
psychotherapy	⊙ psychic therapy
reading the paper	⊙ reading your aura

Notes

1. *The Evening Standard*, 11 December 1996.

2. Today's young women are far more educated than older women. According to the British Household Panel Study almost 27 per cent of women under 25 have A levels and almost 43 per cent have O levels. In contrast, less than 10 per cent of women aged between 35 and 55 have A levels. Less than 30 per cent of these have O levels. The educational achievement of women over 55 is worse still. Less than 4 per cent have A levels and less than 12 per cent have O levels. See Wilkinson H and Mulgan G, 1995, *Freedom's Children: work, relationships and politics for 18-34 year olds in Britain today*, Demos, London.

3. Europeans aged 15 to 24 are almost twice as likely to have visited another European country as those over 25, and the proportion of Europeans who can speak more than two languages has risen from 28 per cent in 1969 to 42 per cent in 1990. Halpern D, 1995, 'Values, morals and modernity: the values, constraints and norms of European youth', in Rutter M and Smith J, eds, 1995, *Psychosocial disorders in young people: time trends and their causes*, John Wiley and Sons, Chichester, 381.

4. Inglehart R, 1990, *Culture shift in advanced industrial society*, Princeton University Press, Princeton. See note 2 (Wilkinson and Mulgan, 1995).

5. This trend was also observed in: see note 2 (Wilkinson and Mulgan, 1995).

6. See for example, Ghazi P and Jones J, 1997, *Getting a life*, Hodder and Stoughton, London. See also Schor J, 1995, 'The new American dream?' in *The time squeeze*, Demos Quarterly issue 5, Demos, London, and 'The only way is down', *The Guardian*, 3 February 1997.

7. Coupland D, 1992, *Generation X*, Abacus, London.

8. Sheehy G, 1996, *New passages: mapping your life across time*, HarperCollins, London.

9. For an interesting sociological study of this phenomenon see, Pahl R, 1996, *After Success*, Polity Press, London.

10. 'Shaping factors' in *Planning for Social Change 1996-97*, vol 1, The Henley Centre, London, 1997.

11. See Pahl R, 1995, 'Finding time to live' in *The time squeeze*, Demos Quarterly issue 5, Demos, London.

12. See for example, Cannon D, 1994, *Generation X and the new work ethic*, Demos, London; Wilkinson H and Bentley T, 1995, *Diversity and change: a case study of young professionals*, Demos, London and also Wilkinson, H, 1995, *Diversity and change: a case study of regional broadcasting*, Demos, London. In these cases, there was a concern about corporate drop out among women high fliers in these organisations but closer quantitative and qualitative analysis suggested that in fact it was as much a problem with young male professionals as with the female professionals.

13. For more on this see the collection of articles in *The time squeeze*, Demos Quarterly issue 5. See note 6. See also, note 2 (Wilkinson and Mulgan, 1995) and also Etzioni A, 1993, *The parenting deficit*, Demos, London.

14. See for a discussion of this issue and solutions to it, Kraemer S, 1995, *Active fathering for the future*, Demos, London.

15. Ferri E and Smith K, 1996, *Parenting in the 1990s*, Family Policy Studies Centre, London.

16. See for example, Cooper C and Lewis S, 1995, *Beyond family friendly organisations*, Demos, London.

17. Survey by the Institute for Employment Studies of 200 freelance translators across the European Union. Cited in *The Guardian*, 28 October 1996.

18. See Marlow S, *Female entrepreneurs – do they mean business?*, ESRC research report, Economic and Social Research Council, London.

19. This expression is borrowed from Rosamund Elwies of GGT Advertising, in a speech given at the Ethical Marketing Conference, 1995.

20. See note 2 (Wilkinson and Mulgan, 1995), 57. Citing figures from the British Household Panel Study, this report showed that 77.4 per cent of professional women under 35 depend on formal child care, compared to only 35.8 per cent of managerial and technical workers and 27.3 per cent of skilled non manual workers.

21. See note 6 (*Time squeeze*, 1995).

22. 'Hearth and soul', *The Daily Telegraph*, 10 December 1996

23. *Which?*, November 1995, 9. Of a sample of 20,000 questionnaires, with 8000 responses, satisfaction rates were as follows: osteopathy, 80 per cent, chiropody, 85 per cent, homeopathy, 75 per cent, acupuncture, 80 per cent, aromatherapy, 90 per cent, reflexology, 81 per cent, herbalist, 78 per cent, hypnotherapy, 49 per cent and healing, 90 per cent.

Masculine values pervade: Mannish Mel

Mannish Mel has grown up in the post-feminist era, inspired by the pioneering women in business and shaped by the example of Britain's first woman prime minister. Mel is not particularly attached to femininity. For her equality means the chance to behave more like men, to enjoy power, excitement and sex. Independent and ambitious, she expects power and success, and is increasingly achieving it. She is more willing to take risks than the older, pinstriped women who laid the groundwork for her opportunities and she is less ideological than a previous generation of feminists.

What are the signs that 'mannish' values will become more prominent? One is the survey evidence that today's teenage girls have already become more 'male' in some of their values than men, being more attached to risk, hedonism, and even violence.[1] By 2010, Mel will be well advanced in her career and will be bringing new values to bear at work, values that differentiate her from earlier generations.

Other signs of masculinisation can be found in popular culture. Celluloid images of the female equivalents of 'new lads' – the 'new ladette' – have been increasingly visible from the mid-1990s. Hollywood has provided us

Mannish Mel

with a string of new macho female role models, such as Sigourney Weaver's Ripley in the Aliens series, a shaven-headed warrior, Jamie Lee Curtis in *Blue steel*, Linda Hamilton in *Terminator 2* and women who enjoy using sex as a tool of power such as Sharon Stone in *Basic instinct*. The comic strip *Tank girl* offered another interpretation – a hard drinking, homicidal and stroppy young woman who is an ironic counter to the Schwarzeneggers and Stallones. Tank Girl isn't just another brawny bimbo: she farts, picks her nose, cuts herself shaving, lives in a rubbish tip and is generally as unfeminine as you can imagine. Her attitude and ambition chime well with a generation of women who have been beating the boys at exams, are increasingly beating them in the job market and who soon may be beating them in the race for top jobs. For Tank Girl, it is appropriate that men don't have much of a role in the future – even her lover is half man, half kangaroo.

Meaning and values: maleness dominates in all areas

Where did this new vision of woman come from? Tomorrow's ladettes have modelled some of their behaviour and values on the previous, pioneering generation of highly educated professional women: women who dressed like men and acted like men in order to succeed in the workplace. This masculinisation was particularly visible in the power dressing, pinstriped suits of the 1980s, and in the joke about Margaret Thatcher: that she was more of a man than the rest of the cabinet put together.

While the strongest signs of masculine values are to be found among teenagers, belief in the power of the individual to succeed and a strong commitment to independence are now widespread: 33 per cent of all women describe themselves as strongly attached to their independence and individuality in 1996.[2] Thirty-one per cent of women in Synergy's survey say that they wouldn't mind being born again as a man. These women are most likely to be under 25 and least likely to be over 65.

Synergy's research suggests several types of masculinised woman. If one group is now still in school and at university, there is also an older group of professional women, aged between 35 and 44 years, who use a masculine managerial style in the workplace, but are also angry and resentful about the glass ceiling. These women are often less than sympathetic to those rising in the ranks behind them,[3] precisely because they have had to make sacrifices en route – studies consistently show that successful career women are less likely to have children and are more likely to be divorced or single.[4] A 1994 survey of television executives found that 70 per cent of women in their thirties were childless compared to 34 per cent of their male colleagues (see chart below).

But increasing numbers of women have been more successful at balancing work and home, without being obviously feminine in their styles of management or their approach to work. Marjorie Scardino recently made news by becoming the first female CEO of a FTSE 100 quoted company, Pearson, with a husband willing to take on

Who has children among TV creative staff

Children	% Men	% Women
None	34	70
One	13	15
Two	34	11
Three	16	2
Four	2	1
Five	1	0

Source: *British film industry/television industry tracking survey*, British Film Institute, London, 1994.

most of the domestic chores. Nicola Horlick from Morgan Grenfell, who hit the headlines because of her high profile sacking, played on the fact that despite being a high flier in a man's world she has managed to bring up five children, but showed no sign of believing that women should be any softer than men. Like their predecessors, these women have succeeded by outshining their male colleagues, perhaps being even more conscientious, thorough and professional than those they had to compete against.

Some of the subsequent generation, now in their twenties, may feel little need to be feminine at all. These are the women who now enjoy boxing and martial arts, driving fast cars and drinking heavily in public. They no longer feel any inhibitions about behaving like lads.[5]

The new optimism

A new mood of optimism among women has contributed to this shift in values away from femininity. A recent study in the USA found that women of all ages thought that women's lives would continue to improve. Older women generally believed that their daughter's generation had far more opportunities.[6] In the UK, we found that 44 per cent of all women interviewed in 1996 by Synergy are optimistic and that younger women are the most optimistic of all.[7]

The women most likely to exude this new optimism are higher educated (ABs), under 35 and in work. Synergy's research also shows that being in work tends to make women more attached to 'masculine' values, seeking power and prestige from work, and hedonism and excitement from leisure. Overall, 31 per cent of women are at ease with flexible and interchangeable gender roles. There is also a close connection between work and an increased sense of self-esteem and self-worth, and for women in work health, appearance and convenience are all important issues.

Many of the factors apparently pushing women towards more masculine values look likely to continue

Mannish Mel's values, 1996

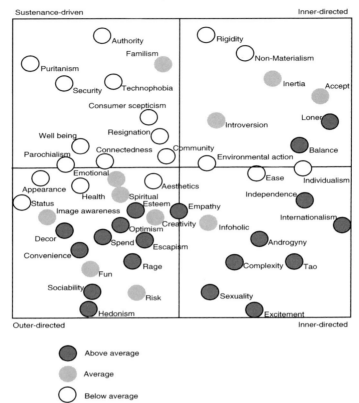

Source: *Insight '96*, Synergy Brand Values Ltd, London, 1977.

over the next twelve years. Higher rates of education, more involvement in creating and running businesses, and more involvement in the workplace and as breadwinners could translate into a further rejection of feminine and maternal roles. In 1996, 14 per cent of women viewed work as a career, important to them personally, and 13 per cent were working to support the family, playing what has traditionally been seen as a male role. Typically C2DEs and primarily aged between 22 and 44, these women form a sizeable proportion of the population and are strongly attached to 'masculine' values.

As the table overleaf shows, the youngest women are becoming strikingly more masculine in their values, with

Chart: Masculine values index

Value	Sex	Age		
		15-17	18-34	35-54
Crude hedonism	female	3.83	1.64	0.45
	male	2.28	1.58	0.67
Seeking success	female	2.44	1.06	0.85
	male	1.91	1.18	0.71
Risk taking	female	2.91	1.57	0.70
	male	1.38	1.58	0.84

Source: *MORI Socioconsult, Freedom's children*, Demos, London, 1995.

15 to 17 year olds strongly attached to hedonism, success and risk.

The sheer weight of numbers looks set to increase the social acceptability of masculine values. In 1995, there were already more female professionals under 35 than over and each generation has been substantially more educated than the previous one.[8] The map on the previous page shows the values that Mannish Mel in her younger incarnation is increasingly attached to, and Synergy's analysis confirms that these values are hardening with each new age cohort.[9]

Women's new found optimism and assertiveness doesn't just show up in surveys, it also has a chemical component. Research shows that the social environment is crucial in determining serotonin levels, which are linked to depression.[10] Historically women have tended to suffer higher reported levels of depression than men and they have been the most frequent users of anti-depressants and tranquillisers. But women's serotonin levels are now rising. By 2010, depression and Prozac could have become a thing of the past as women's changing character raises serotonin levels to an all-time high. Perhaps by then, depression among men will be widespread and men will have displaced women as the most prolific pill poppers.

The new triumphalism

Optimism is breeding a sense of superiority, even triumphalism. Forty per cent of women in Synergy's survey agreed that women were naturally superior to men, with a hard core – 6 per cent – strongly believing this to be true. Interestingly, the great majority of this core were younger.

Mel at work in 2010 – giving as good as she gets and more

In this more masculine incarnation, tomorrow's women will be capitalising on their greater achievement over men at all levels of education,[11] across all age groups and social classes[12] and in all areas of work. A growing proportion will be in supervisory and team leader positions in the predominantly service-based economy, while women managers and professionals will be nearing parity with men.

The proportion of women in the workforce has increased steadily over the past couple of decades.[13] If male values continue to spread, women will increasingly devote their energies to work. By 2010 the average length of maternity leave, currently less than a year for two thirds of women,[14] could have become even shorter as Mannish Mel throws off the constraints of motherhood by returning to work as soon as possible (or by avoiding motherhood altogether).

Having thoroughly absorbed masculine values, she will also eschew the drop in status and lack of opportunity that part-time and contract work so often led to in the 1990s. While in 1995, women constituted 85 per cent of part-time workers,[15] this may be nearer 50 per cent in 2010, partly because men, increasingly displaced from high status jobs by tougher and more confident women, will be forced into secondary positions in the service economy, adapting through necessity to forms of work which were unattractive to them in the late 1990s. There is already evidence of this as men move into service and semi-skilled manufacturing jobs that used to be dominated by women and as they begin to complain about discriminatory barriers keeping them out.[16]

Business feminism triumphs
Mannish Mel will combine optimism and self-esteem with rage and she will put her anger to effective use. Seventeen per cent of women in 1996 say that they don't get mad, they get even. Discrepancies in pay levels will have disappeared as a result of endless battles fought in courts and through union negotiations in the early years of the twenty first century. Mel will also benefit from the fact that women are more numerous in legal professions, and are keen to use the law to further women's interests and correct past injustices.

In 2010, feminism at work will be becoming a thing of the past, the preserve of lower socio-economic groups (primarily Ds, if at all) because tomorrow's women will be so confident in their success, so truly mannish and so numerous in the workplace in the key decision making roles, that they will no longer need to band together with other women to form pressure groups in the workplace such as Forum UK and the City Women's Network which existed in 1997.[17] The promise of Naomi Wolf's book, *Fire with fire*,[18] in which women exercise economic power and muscle on their own behalf in the 'civil war of gender', will have been realised.

Winner takes all and increasingly women are winning
Mannish Mel will succeed in the upper echelons of the commercial world, attaining equal representation with men in the boardroom.[19] In the fiercely competitive global environment of 2010, women's attitudes to work will have become more male.[20] A recent survey of women running small businesses found that they were autocratic in their management style, operating with fewer levels of authority, and fewer written rules with most information stored in their head. Nearly 63 per cent said that they operate with no delegation of authority compared to 48 per cent of men.[21] *Changing lives* data shows that the

attitudes of full-time working women towards trends such as globalisation, technology and management are already more like men than those of other women. In the 1990s there are also indications that younger women will be more preoccupied with the factors that will affect their ability to succeed economically. Mel won't have any qualms about exploiting third world women in factories overseas and will be tough on her less educated, less confident and less ambitious female workers.

Enjoying power and preferring to succeed in a hierarchical structure, Mannish Mel is not concerned with women's issues or universal advancement. She relishes proving herself in a man's world and believes that with hard work and application any woman can do the same. In 2010 Mel will think nothing of working long hours. By 1995, young women professionals were already the hardest workers of all,[22] and in the fast-paced global business environment of the twenty first century, where time is money, Mel is unlikely to want to waste time having lunch. Instead she will increasingly save time by relying on 'complete nutrition' food tablets which are expected to be fully developed in the first quarter of the next century, reserving cooking and eating out for weekends. 'Juggling'

Full-time working women's attitudes more similar to men than other women

Percentage giving as reasons for unemployment	Men	Women	F/T
Effects of technology	51	47	48
Bad management	37	29	37
Employee productivity	9	6	9
Excessive wage claims	12	16	12

Source: *Changing lives 1986-1996*, AGB Taylor Nelson/Future Foundation, London.

women will do what they can to buy back time spent on shopping, cooking and eating.

In this scenario, women will comprise some 50 per cent of the armed forces and police recruits, having overcome the widespread discrimination in these uniformed services that has been well publicised both here and in the United States.[23] Women are already entering the police force and army in greater numbers than ever before, and they will benefit from rising qualifications requirements and greater dependence on technology rather than physical strength. For the same reasons, women will make up 50 per cent of entrants to other male dominated professions such as pilots, heavy engineering and fire fighting.

Men beware!
Confident, expressive and enjoying the power that they have acquired through years of persistent battling, the new ladettes will have beaten men at their own game in the workplace. Men in turn will increasingly think of themselves as victims.[24] Complaints of job discrimination by men already exceeded those made by women in 1995 and 1996[25] and will have become more numerous by 2010 as high flying women recruit career women and employ men in lowly occupations.

Power will itself prove to be the ultimate aphrodisiac. These themes were explored in the mid 1990s film *Disclosure* whose story centred around a tough female executive who turns the tables on her anxious, middle aged male colleague, and delights in sexually harassing him. Accusations of sexual harassment of men by women will have increased to some 30 per cent of all cases and male secretaries will have become status symbols in the workplace.

Critical consumers in 2010 – wealth and power
If we project forward from current trends, where women are already the principal earners in 20 per cent of households compared to just 6.6 per cent in the early

1980s,[26] by 2010, three in five women will be earning more than their partners. In some cases, particularly in the mid socio-economic range, C1C2, where Demos' research shows that women are already more ambitious and oriented to success than their male counterparts,[27] they will actually have displaced male breadwinners, and their partners will be relegated to the status of house husband. However, many if not most of these women will be single.

By 2010 more of these women will have eschewed large corporations which don't change quickly enough,[28] and will instead have struck out on their own to achieve the status and success which they believe is their birthright. The appeal of this view is suggested in contemporary soap operas: Bianca Jackson of *EastEnders* and Jackie Dixon on *Brookside* both have their own businesses while their brothers are aimless and unemployed.

By 2010, some 50 per cent of small businesses will be owned by women. In the USA women-owned businesses already employ more people than the whole of the Fortune 500, with sales exceeding $1 billion in 49 metropolitan districts.[29]

By 2010 women – especially C1s and C2s – will still want to exert their power as consumers in an outer-directed, status oriented sense, and there is already evidence that marketers and advertisers are beginning to take women's consumer power seriously through a feminisation of advertising and communication.

Car advertising is a good example. In 1991, Ford set up the Ford Women's Marketing Panel and female employees from ten countries are now involved in the research, development and evaluation of new vehicles.[30] Adverts for the Peugeot 106 depict two women driving across the desert, *Thelma and Louise* style, while the 'ask before you borrow it' campaign for the Nissan Micra shows a man in jeans clutching his crotch having driven his girlfriend's car without her permission. A Volkswagen advert depicted a professional woman celebrating her divorce rather than her marriage. Women already buy half of all new and used cars, and make the final decision in 80 per cent of car sales overall. Twenty-nine per cent of women have bought a car in the past two years.[31]

The challenge of developing media to reach these audiences will have been met by 2010. Magazines will continue to proliferate and multiply for women's audiences (alongside more men's titles based on the model of women's ones).[32] Rather than losing their knowledge and skill as consumers, women in 2010 will be more demanding than ever: top of their list of requirements will be time saving and convenience as they spend longer at work. Experience at work will have made them as technologically confident as their male counterparts and among younger cohorts this process of equalisation will have started at school. Research conducted for BT by the Henley Centre showed that 48 per cent of women at work believe that their experience of using the telephone at work has made them more confident as a teleconsumer, compared to 29 per cent of men.[33]

Mannish Mel will be an avid teleshopper and user of electronic means of accessing goods and services in 2010. Direct distribution will make up some 30 per cent of retail activity, and by then all the major grocery multiples will have established efficient automatic ordering services with evening deliveries to satisfy Mel's requirements. Gourmet meals on wheels could become commonplace, making eating in for dual working households a gourmet treat and taking the hard work out of hosting dinner parties. Logging onto the Room Service website with your postcode already offers the quick route to ordering high class Chinese, Italian, Thai, Japanese and other cuisines within the hour. Black tie 'butlers' will deliver the food piping hot and will even stop at the off licence on the way. Convenience will no longer need to mean compromise.[34]

Increased spending power will also make women more attractive in traditionally male markets – financial services, cars and technology. We have seen the impact of Ford's first female designer in the appealing KA. Already banks are introducing more flexible, female-orientated products, such as the Bank of Ireland's 'lifestyle mortgage' and women's pension plans are now being advertised in the pages of *Marie Claire* and *Options*.[35]

Mannish Mel will have lost interest in changing the world and exerting pressure on companies to make their products or personnel policies more women-friendly. Already there is some evidence from the *Changing lives* study that the most radical and angry consumers among women are more traditional, older mothers while the attitudes of younger and full-time working women's attitudes are more like those of their male counterparts.

Party time: girls just wanna have fun!
Tomorrow's ladettes will work hard and play hard. By the year 2010, the Spice Girls, the first of many highly successful all female pop acts will be 35 and still going strong. Mel B will be an icon of the new ladettes who emerged in the late 1990s but have refused to roll over and grow up in their thirties. They will still be loud, sexy and will enjoy their beer. Television programmes like the *Girlie show* will have set the pace for a slew of programmes encouraging women to behave badly.

In 2010 Mel will not be sitting at home knitting or dressmaking – the proportion of women doing this fell by 10 per cent between 1983 and 1993 while at the same time the proportion doing DIY rose from 24 to 30 per cent.[36] Among the younger age group the main recipe that Mel will follow is the age-old male concoction of football, fags and fornication advocated in men's magazines like *Loaded* in the 1990s.

There is already substantial evidence that with greater economic independence the gender gap in leisure patterns is closing. Already one quarter of football fans are women and women's participation in male sports – football, boxing and shooting is increasing significantly,[37] partly because younger women, especially those aged 15 to 17 are taking as much pleasure in violence as boys.[38]

Working women will also have closed the gender gap

in drinking. In one study 79 per cent of single women had visited a pub in the last three months – closer to the 83 per cent of single men than the 59 per cent of other women. And while men's drinking has been relatively stable, there has been a continued increase in women's drinking,[39] partly because the proportion of women exceeding alcohol limits rises steadily with income (full-time working women are twice as likely to exceed the sensible limits as women who do not work or work part time).[40] Women are also smoking more at a time when male consumption has stabilised. Among 16 to 24 year old women regular smoking has increased by 5 per cent since 1994.[41]

Mannish Mel is instrumental in her relationships with members of opposite sex, just as men have been in the past. More casual sex and more transactional attitudes look likely. At the top end of the market, professional male escort services will be thriving for professional women on business trips in a classic inversion of gender roles.[42] Lower down the socio-economic scale, the Chippendales will have spawned a new strand of female entertainment ranging from male stripogrammes and bottomless male dancers to toy boys in pinnies serving in restaurants. Female porn magazines, racy novels and virtual reality dating games will also have proliferated.

Mannish Mel at home – the birth of tank girl?
At home, Mannish Mel's entry into the workplace has resulted in a more even distribution of domestic chores between the sexes, continuing a long term trend, which has been tracked consistently by Professor Jonathon Gershuny at Essex University.[43] Intriguingly, this is another instance of women adopting male standards. As the following table shows, there has been a rapid closing of the gender gap, which we expect to have almost disappeared by 2010 – partly because women are simply choosing to spend less time on domestic chores,[44] and more time at work. This 'dirty generation' will be in their mid to late thirties by 2010 – and will by then be able to

afford to buy technologies to do work for them – like smart cleaner robots.

Others will still opt for the personal touch. In the 1980s and 1990s we have seen a dramatic growth in the domestic service economy to the extent that Mintel, the market research organisation, estimates that there are already more nannies than car workers in Britain.[45] While the figures are impossible to quantify accurately, recent headlines have suggested that the richest 10 per cent are now using the poorest 10 per cent more and more as servants.[46] The two fastest areas of jobs growth are professional and administrative posts on the one hand, and personal and protective services on the other. Many women will be found in both categories. The latter contains 2.75 million people, more than work in factories, and is expected to grow by 4 per cent each year. It will

The dirty generation? Hours spent on housework each week

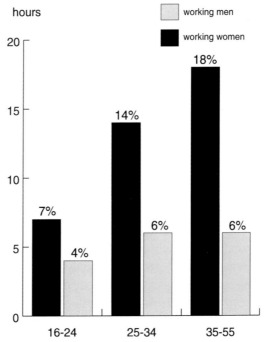

Source: *British household panel study, Freedom's children*, Demos, London, 1995.

include many working as servants to hard working and hard living women like Mel.

Does Mannish Mel want or need a family?

Today's trends towards later childbearing, cohabiting rather than marriage, and remaining single, could become more marked. The growing desire for balanced sources of satisfaction from 1986 to 1996 in the *Changing lives* study (see chart overleaf) could presage a further future shift away from the home. Indeed all age groups show a significant increase over this ten year period.

Long distance love

Single life is becoming more appealing[47] and more people are opting for intimacy at a distance. For women who value their independence too much to bother themselves with families or involved relationships, the advent of flat-rate phone calls (one set charge wherever you call in the world, rather like the Internet) could enable long distance romances to prosper. Coupled with increasingly competitive international airfares for snatched holidays, this could be the perfect arrangement for ambitious work-centred women. Supersonic flight could soon be more accessible – at the moment it costs ten times as much as subsonic flight but the price gap is predicted to shrink dramatically.[48]

Mel's increasing power at work could prove to be an aphrodisiac. Good quality sex will be high on her checklist and she will be seeking companionship in the arms of younger, less powerful men who find her success and power attractive. Many will be prepared to buy sex, just as men have done in the past. Male prostitution, especially at the upmarket end, will be thriving.[49]

Child-free women

One fifth of women born since the 1960s are expected to choose to remain childless,[50] and by 2010 the proportion may have risen as high as 30 per cent.[51] As more women opt out of motherhood, one surprising effect will be to

Women continue to seek satisfaction outside the home

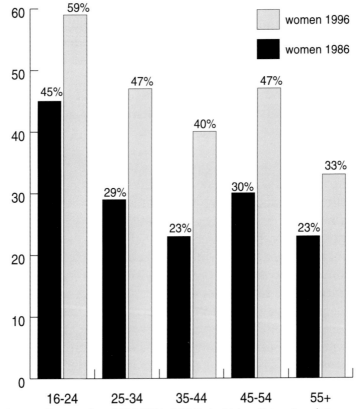

% agreeing they
get equal satisfaction
from home and work

women 1996

women 1986

16-24   25-34   35-44   45-54   55+

Source: *Changing lives 1986-1996*, AGB Taylor Nelson/Future Foundation, London.

reduce the pressures on companies to provide childcare and parental leave.

Managing motherhood
However, women will also have more choice over whether and when to have children. The trend to later childrearing, which is already well established,[52] is supported by medical advances that are making it more practical for women to have children in their forties and fifties. The very wealthy will benefit from surrogate

motherhood. Medical science is already narrowing the gap between beginning and preserving human life, and this could in turn lead to foetal development entirely outside the body, with foetuses going from test tubes to incubators (which are now used to support babies as young as twenty weeks): a form of maternity that would cause scarcely a ripple in a busy schedule.[53]

A forthcoming Mintel report estimates that we are spending over £4 billion per year on nannies to fill the parenting deficit.[54] By 2010 we expect this to have substantially increased but Mel will also be keen to rely on the latest technologies. Rather than choosing to telecommute, Mel will teleparent – as many parents already do.

Politics, power and world view: women succeed but not to transform

Mel is a post-feminist and somewhat schizophrenic in her politics. She is instinctively Thatcherite, believing in un-regulated, open markets and free competition in all areas. At the same time, she has thoroughly imbibed feminist ideas and wants the chance to even the score with men.

She is not a political activist by any stretch of the imagination and sees politics as boring. Younger women are already less party political than older women and less likely to be active in single issues, even on issues such as the environment.[55] Today only 3 per cent of women are members of political parties, but the figure could be even lower in 2010 as workplace issues absorb more time and energies.[56]

Many women's organisations will have closed down, or faced a significant haemorrhaging of support, and when women do become involved it will be more to help their careers and to access valuable networks than because of any sense of altruism or sisterhood.[57] Communities will suffer from the loss of women's time, which used to hold them together. Reports of shortages of Brown Owls because of the 'time squeeze' in working women's lives will have become commonplace by 2010.[58]

If Mel votes at all it will be a matter of self-interest: she will be looking to see which party offers the best chance of a rising disposable income and which is least likely to constrain her in meeting her desires. And while, through sheer ambition and determination, the number of female MPs will be around 50 per cent, they will be content to have succeeded in a male dominated world and will not be a force for radical change. The majority of these 320 women MPs may be relatively young, childless, and small 'c' conservative: perhaps instead of campaigning for family-friendly working hours and a creche they will by then be campaigning for a bigger gun club.

The one area of politics where Mannish Mel will be assertive is in protecting her hard won reproductive rights. Because she values her freedom, she will stand up for choice against the growing pro-life lobby,[59] and will support technologists finding new ways to give women control over reproduction.

Mannish Mel's uncertain futures

Male crisis and the Back to Basics backlash

If in the 1980s gender politics was dominated by Margaret Thatcher, a woman who often acted more like a man, in the late 1990s and early 2000s they could be dominated by men trying to be more like women – complaining about their oppression, their status as victims and how the world is conspiring against them.[60] Men are now actively campaigning for positive action and discrimination in schools and at work. By 2010 there could be a much fiercer reaction against women who are seen to be emasculating men. This backlash would be fuelled by many factors: weakened families, rising financial demands on fathers, the public safety fears caused by aimless, dissolute young men and unease about women's more visible hedonism.

Some of these tensions could have important political effects. Already in the 1990s there are some evident strains in the Conservative Party between its entrepreneurial and individualistic wing and the more traditional, socially conservative wing. By 2010 the two could have split. One, the Enterprise Party would appeal to women like Mel: it would favour personal freedoms, lower taxes, and would include many prominent successful women. The other, the England Party would be nationalistic, anti-European and socially conservative, and would be aiming through laws and incentives to encourage women back into the home.

A complete crisis of masculine values
The other uncertainty concerns the sustainability of masculine values. Despite mannish women's advances in the world of work, in the 1980s and 1990s many women have been actively questioning the values of the corporate world, voting with their feet and leaving large organisations in favour of self-employment in order to achieve greater balance in their lives.[61] Many women succeeding in business do not simply copy men's values. Research by Barclays Bank[62] among women who have started their own businesses, for example, found that only 15 per cent are motivated simply by money. In general, the desire for fulfilment is now more important for men and women, standing at 38 per cent and 34 per cent respectively, with an overall convergence over the last ten years as the chart on the next page shows. This pattern of convergence is clearest among younger men and women (see chart on page 109).

The signs of a convergence between men's and women's values could push strongly against 'mannish' values, masculine management styles and the emphasis on work to the exclusion of everything else. Interestingly, older female managers in their thirties, forties and fifties are already attracting criticism from younger men and women who are seeking a more balanced life.[63] While younger men are becoming more feminised,[64] older men in their forties and fifties, who having sacrificed their personal lives on the altar of career success, are now questioning whether it was worth it.[65]

Men and women increasingly want the same things

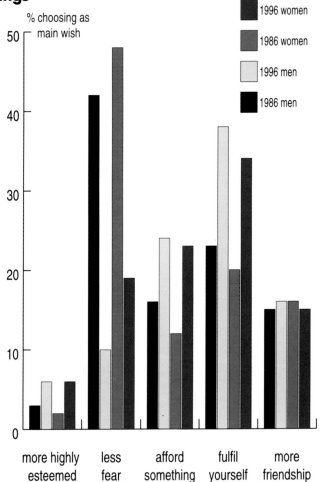

% choosing as main wish

Legend:
- 1996 women
- 1986 women
- 1996 men
- 1986 men

Categories: more highly esteemed · less fear · afford something · fulfil yourself · more friendship

Source: *Changing lives 1986-1996*, AGB Taylor Nelson/Future Foundation, London.

Mel suffers the male diseases of the past

What if Mel herself turns away from masculine values, questioning whether they help her to lead a fulfilled life? Stress, already worse for women in the 1990s, may have reached crisis point before 2010, unless Mel finds ways of dealing with it more effectively. A recent Reuters report, *Dying for information* highlighted the additional stress that female executives suffer in the workplace – 41 per cent of women compared to 30 per cent of men believe that they need more information to keep pace with colleagues. Fifty-six per cent of women managers claim to suffer ill health because they do not have time for diet or exercise.[66] The *Changing lives* data shows that most women are concerned to stay fit and healthy above all else and that this is as important for working women as others, but the pressures of stressful careers on time inevitably make it hard to keep fit. Short of time, Mel's tendency may be to relieve stress by smoking and drinking just as men have

Young men and women increasingly want the same things

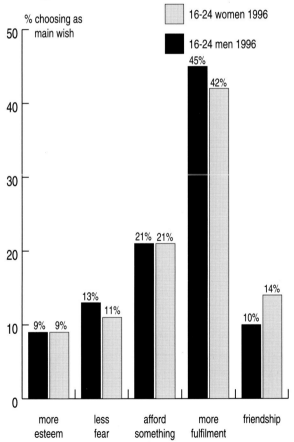

Source: *Changing lives 1996*, AGB Taylor Nelson/Future Foundation, London.

done in the past. As we have seen, there is a clear correlation between the continued increase in women's drinking and the rising numbers of full-time, single working women.[67]

Mel will also become vulnerable to the male diseases of the past. Increased smoking and other associated lifestyle diseases from stress – heart attacks, strokes and the like – will have become more common, and the gender gap in women's health may even be going into reverse – already death rates from lung cancer and pulmonary disease are increasing among women. To this heady and unhealthy cocktail may be added the stress of being the main breadwinner. Although men are still more afraid of unemployment across the age groups, women under 25 are fast closing the gap, as the chart opposite shows.

Women may also suffer from weaker personal support networks, having sacrificed friends and family to the pursuit of careers. Across the world, women's financial independence tends to correlate with increasing divorce rates and this in turn tends to lead to more depression. For those who avoid relationships things may not be any better. Already in the 1990s, surveys show that single people are more likely to suffer depression, to drink heavily and to think about committing suicide.[68] Professional escort services may boost Mel's outward status, but they won't fill the emotional void in her life, any more than prostitutes have for men.

In the 1980s and 1990s Hollywood began to portray career women as unhinged and unhappy – witness Glenn Close in *Fatal attraction* and Demi Moore in *Disclosure*. Mannish Mel in her new incarnation may well be questioning whether being one of the boys is exacting too high a price on her overall well-being – not least perhaps in the need for psychotherapy.

Parental fulfilment
Like contemporary fathers, more women in the future may come to regret not devoting more time to parenting. Germaine Greer has publicly regretted her decision not to

Fear of unemployment

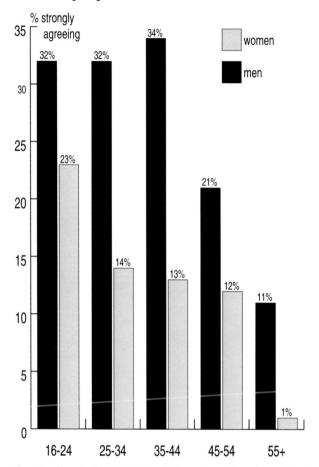

Source: *Changing lives 1996*, AGB Taylor Nelson/Future Foundation, London.

have children and Dr Miriam Stoppard has commented that she wished that she had made more time for her children when they were young.[69] Research for Parents at Work found that 64 per cent felt they did not see enough of their children and as many as three-quarters of women reported not having enough time for themselves.[70]

The irony, then, is that the great confidence and success of women like Mel could also bring with it guilt and unhappiness. If she does have children she will be more aware than previous generations about the emotional needs of developing children and their need for quantity as well as quality time. If she does not have children she may feel that she is missing out on one of the biggest sources of potential fulfilment. This version of the future looks strongly supported by current trends. But in the long run it may not be sustainable, a cul-de-sac rather than a highway to power and satisfaction.

Signs of the times

getting mad	⊙ getting even
power dressing	⊙ powering up
one of the boys	⊙ girl power
stiletto heels	⊙ flick knife weals
mine's a Perrier	⊙ mine's a pint
single mothers	⊙ single households
Schwarzenegger and Stallone	⊙ Thelma and Louise
a nice little runner	⊙ eight cylinder engines
sisterhood	⊙ girls in the 'hood
hot flushes	⊙ HRT
in the margins	⊙ profit margins
depression	⊙ hedonism
bread maker	⊙ bread winner
cross your heart bra	⊙ Wonder bra
nice girls	⊙ Spice girls
patriarchy	⊙ hierarchy
knitting	⊙ hitting
pin-striped suits	⊙ Dr Marten Boots
Baywatch babe	⊙ Tank Girl
Bunny girls	⊙ Chippendale boys
quality of life	⊙ performance related pay
shopping trip	⊙ power trip
married to Mr Right	⊙ married to the company
waiting by the 'phone	⊙ phoning tonight's male escort
ringside seat	⊙ boxing clever
Country Casuals	⊙ casual sex
houseproud gender	⊙ dirty generation
childbearing	⊙ cohabiting
Richard Branson	⊙ Patsy Bloom
equal opportunities	⊙ business opportunities
housewife	⊙ househusband

Notes

1. For a detailed analysis of this see Wilkinson H and Mulgan G, 1995, *Freedom's children: work, relationships and politics for 18-34 year olds in Britain today*, Demos, London.

2. These women are creative, optimistic and have high levels of self esteem. They are also committed to flexible and interchangeable gender roles, and are most numerous among the 35 to 54 year olds. Some of these women experience their lives as loners, although they are relatively accepting of this. Some can be quite brittle and rigid in their world view.

3. Dr Marilyn Davidson of UMIST identifies the 'queen bee syndrome', which she labels women who have put work before family, have made it through the glass ceiling and are then unsympathetic to other women coming up behind them. 'Monster raving loony bosses', *The Guardian*, 10 June 1996.

4. Davidson M J and Cooper C, 'Female managers in Britain: a comparative perspective' in *Human Resources Management*, Summer 1987, vol 26 no 2, 221-223; Davidson M and Cooper C, 'Executive woman under pressure' in *International Review of Applied Psychology*, vol 35; Lewis, S and Cooper C, 'The stress of combined occupational and parental roles, a review of the literature' in *British Psychological Society*, 1983. Coe T, 1992, *The key to the men's club*, Institute of Management, London.

5. See for example, Denfeld R, 1997, *Kill the body, the head will fall*, Warner books, New York.

6. *Women: the new providers*, The Whirlpool Foundation, Benton Harbor, Michigan, 1995.

7. This new optimism among younger women was first reported on in Wilkinson H, 1994, *No turning back: generations and the genderquake*, Demos, London. It has been confirmed by our analysis of the 1996 Insight survey.

8. For these figures and many more see note 1 (Wilkinson and Mulgan, 1995).

9. Synergy's research suggests that today's under 25 year olds are even more optimism, than 25 to 34 year olds. Drawing on the time trends data, Synergy's analysis suggests that these trends are cumulative and are not simply the product of life-stage and socio-economic status.

10. Women who are most likely to be depressed have three or more children, have minimal social support, lost a parent before the age of fourteen and have a low income. In one large survey 100 per cent of women with all four of these risk factors were depressed. 'Up on a higher level', *Independent on Sunday*, 18 August 1996.

11. Barber M, 1993, *Young people and their attitudes to school: an interim report of a research project*, Centre for Successful Schools, Keele University, Keele, 6-8. He argues that a major educational issue for the future is the under achievement of boys.

12. Social classes DE are the exception to this.

13. The proportion of women as a percentage of the total workforce rose from 35 per cent in 1960 to 49 per cent in 1993. The Economist, 1993, *Pocket Britain in figures*, Penguin, London, 83. In five years time women will constitute 51 per cent of employees in Britain. 'Women at work', *The Independent*, 3 December 1996.

14. Wilkinson H, and Briscoe I, 1996, *Parental Leave: the price of family values?*, Demos, London, 8.

15. Central Statistical Office, 1995, *Social trends*, HMSO, London, 59.

16. Out of every ten jobs being created at the moment 9.7 are in services. Statistics and analysis prepared by Paul Gregg at the London School of Economics for the Barass TV company series *Genderquake*, broadcast on Channel 4, June 1996.

17. The idea of business feminism is explored in Wilkinson H, 1996, 'Business feminism' in *The new enterprise culture*, Demos Quarterly issue 8, Demos, London.

18. Wolf, N, 1994, *Fire with fire: the new female power and how it will change the twenty first century*, Chatto and Windus, London.

19. In August 1989, 21 companies (11 per cent) of the then Times Top 200 companies had women on their boards, by 1993 the figure was 49 (25 per cent), an increase of 127 per cent. Over the same period the number of women directors increased by over 100 per cent from 24 to 51. Holton V, Rabbetts J and Scrivener S, 1993, *Women on the boards of Britain's top 200 companies: a progress report*, Ashridge Management Research Group, Berkhamstead.

20. For more on this convergence of attitudes between younger men and women in relation to work see note 1 (Wilkinson and Mulgan, 1995).

21. See 'Women who make a difference', *Financial Times*, 18 February 1997.

22. See note 1 (Wilkinson and Mulgan, 1995), 28. These figures come from the British household panel study.

23. There has been an increase in the percentage of female recruits to the army from 8 per cent of total intake in 1976 to 11 per cent in 1996. Figures from the Ministry of Defence

24. Wilkinson, H, 'Call yourself a man or a victim?', *The Independent,* 2 January 1996.

25. In 1995, 820 men and 803 women made complaints to the Equal Opportunities Commission. 'Fem and us', *The Guardian*, 7 May 1996.

26. See note 1, (Wilkinson and Mulgan, 1995), 36.

27. See note 1 (Wilkinson and Mulgan,1995), 30. While women's values are becoming more masculine, men's values are becoming feminised, attached to values seen as more 'soft' and 'caring'.

28. During the 1980s women's self employment rose by 81 per cent, compared with 51 per cent for men. Department of Education and Employment, 1996, *Employment and education: key facts on women factsheet*, HMSO, London. Nearly one third of people setting up their own business through the Business Start Up Scheme are women. See note 17.

29. Bridges W, 1995, *Jobshift*, Allen and Unwin, London, 118.

30. 'Fab gear', *The Guardian*, 26 June 1996.

31. RAC figures cited in 'Baby you can drive my car', *The Independent*, 17 March 1997.

32. Figures cited in: *Media futures 1994-1995*, Henley Centre, London, 1995.

33. *Teleculture futures 1996*, Henley Centre, London, 1996.

34. 'Eat out in style without leaving your home', *The Daily Telegraph*, 10 December 1996.

35. 'Taking account of women's financial needs', *The Guardian*, 2 September 1995.

36. See note 15, 54.

37. Figures from a recent FA premier league survey. 'Falling in love with football', *The Observer*, 13 August 1995. Membership of the National Rifle Association is also increasing. Women currently form 6 per cent of the total membership. Of new members in 1993, 9 per cent were women, and in 1995, 8 per cent were. Figures provided by the National Rifle Association, 1995.

38. See note 1, Wilkinson H and Mulgan G, 1995, 33. In this study 13 per cent of 18 to 24 year old women agreed with the statement 'it's acceptable to use physical violence to get what you want'. Among 15 to 17 year olds, girls had overtaken boys in their attachment to violence as measured by MORI Socioconsult's 'pleasure in violence' index.

39. The proportion of women drinking over the limit has risen steadily from 9 per cent in 1984 to 13 per cent in 1994. Men's drinking has remained stable over this period. Information unit factsheet on alcohol consumption, Alcohol Concern, London, 1994.

40. See note 36, 43.

41. Health Education Authority news release from unpublished material, 10 December, 1996.

42. See for example, 'All in a night's work', *The Guardian*, 21 March 1994. This article found that many women seeking male escorts are career women, frequently married, and often seeking company and sex on business trips. See also Wellings, K, Field J, Johnson A and Wadsworth J, 1994, *Sexual behaviour in Britain*, Penguin, London. Ten per cent of

women aged between 25 to 34 had had more than ten partners compared to just 4 per cent in their mothers' generation.

43. Gershuny J, 1997, 'Time for the family' in *Prospect*, London, 56-57.

44. The ratio of time spent by working women relative to men in cooking, cleaning and doing the laundry has fallen from 3 among 35 to 55 year olds to 2.3 for 25 to 34 year olds and 1.75 for 16 to 24 year olds. Figures from the British household panel study. See note 1 (Wilkinson and Mulgan, 1995), 76.

45. In the UK spending on domestic services rose five times in the last decade to over £3 billion. 'Demos index: facts on the world of work' in *The end of unemployment: bringing work to life*, Demos Quarterly issue 2, Demos, London, 23.

46. 'Give us this day our daily', *The Guardian*, 14 January 1997.

47. *Pre-family lifestyles: young, free and single or couples with commitments?*, Mintel International Group Ltd, London, 1996.

48. Pescovitz D and Wieners B, 1996, *Reality check*, Hardwired Books, San Francisco.

49. See for example, 'All in a night's work', *The Guardian*, 21 March 1994.

50. *Social focus on women*, Central Statistical Office, London, 1995, 16.

51. A report analysing the number of children born to creative staff in the TV industries found that as many as a third of women were childless. *British film industry/television industry tracking survey*, British Film, Institute, London, 1994.

52. There has been a 33 per cent increase in the number of women having children in their forties in the past decade. And for the first time, more babies are now being born to women in their early thirties and in their early twenties. See for example, Babb P, 1995, 'Fertility of the over forties' in Central Statistical Office, *Population trends*, OPCS, London and note 36, 15. This prediction was made in the *Family Policy Studies Centre Bulletin*, April 1995, Family Policy Studies Centre, London.

53. See note 48.

54. 'Home help booms in £4.3 billion nanny state', *Daily Mail*, 12 December 1997.

55. See note 1 (Wilkinson and Mulgan, 1995), 103.

56. See note 15.

57. Grant J, 1995, *Where have all the women gone?: the experience of women aged between 18-34 in women's organisations*, Demos, London.

58. *Time squeeze*, Demos Quarterly issue 5, Demos, London. See also Marrin M, 'Why are we too busy to be Brown Owls?', *The Sunday Telegraph*, 22 October 1995.

59. In the 1990s one in five pregnancies ends in a termination in the UK today. 'Is abortion a vote-winner ?', *The Guardian*, 2 January 1997

60. For more on this see, Wilkinson H, 'Call yourself a man or a victim?', *The Independent*, 1 January 1996.

61. See for example, *National management remuneration survey*, Institute of Management, London, 1994. Roger Young, Director of the Institute of Management was quoted at the time as saying that 'some women could be reacting against the non family friendly policies of larger companies and opting to leave behind the stresses of corporate life for the buzz of being in control of their own companies.'

62. 'Women in business' in *Barclays Review*, Barclays Bank plc, Small Businesses Services, November 1996, London.

63. See for example, Wilkinson H, 1995, *Equality and diversity in a time of change: a case-study of regional broadcasting*, Demos, London. Wilkinson H and Bentley T, 1995; *Equality and diversity in a time of change: a case-study of young professionals*, Demos, London and Wilkinson H, Mattinson D and Cooke V, 1995, *Continuity and change among 18-34 year olds: a qualitative research study*, Demos, London.

64. See for example, Wilkinson H, 1994, *No turning back: generations and the genderquake*, Demos, London and note 1.

65. See Pahl R, 1996, *After success*, Polity Press, London. Professor Cary Cooper of UMIST has also observed this trend.

66. *Dying for information*, Reuters, London, 1996.

67. Women working full time are almost twice as likely to exceed the sensible limits as women who do not work or who work part time. In women the proportion drinking over the limit has risen steadily from 9 per cent in 1984 to 13 per cent in 1994. Men's drinking has remained stable over this period. *Information unit fact sheet on alcohol consumption*, Alcohol Concern, London, 1996.

68. A recent survey in the UK found that single people were more likely to say that they suffered loneliness, depression and ill-health than couples in relationships. 'Singles at risk from drinking and suicide' , *The Independent*, 28 October 1996. A study by Glenn Stanton found that the married consistently show lower mortality rates than the single, widowed or divorced. Stanton G, 1995, *Only a piece of paper?: The unquestionable benefits of lifelong marriage*, Research report, Public Policy Division, Colorado Springs. Cited in Maley B, 1996, *Wedlock and well-being*, Centre for Independent Studies, Sydney.

69. 'Superwoman', *The Evening Standard*, 16 January 1997.

70. Figure provided by Parents at Work, 1996, London.

Return to tradition: Back to Basics Barbara

Back to Basics Barbara has felt for a long time that the world is moving against her. She blames many of society's ills – feckless fathers, babies on benefit, redundant young men or career crazy divorcees – on the 1960s. But she now senses that the tide may be turning in her favour.

Barbara is loosely modelled on one of TV's most popular matriarchs, Barbara Windsor, who plays Peggy Mitchell in *EastEnders*, long suffering mother to her wayward brood (a very different character to some of her earlier incarnations). She is older and typically poorer than the other groups we have described. She works in unskilled jobs if at all, believes in traditional gender roles and is defined by her commitment to her family. The gender revolution of the 1970s passed her by and she is suspicious of those women who have benefited from it. She identifies with one of the most popular TV advertisements among women: the Oxo ad featuring a beleaguered, but happy mother who cooks traditional dinners for her family.[1]

Seventy-five per cent of women over 55 are strongly attached to what Synergy call the 'prudent and proper' cluster, and most are not in work. Believing in traditional, sustenance-driven values, Back to Basics Barbara has fixed

Back to Basics Barbara

puritanical views and finds the complexity and pace of change profoundly destabilising. She identifies with her local neighbourhood and community life, and feels that society has become too materialistic. She would like to bring back the standards that made Britain great. For her, deference to tradition and authority are key. In stark contrast to Naomi, Angela and Mel, Barbara is pessimistic and resigned to her fate.

It would be easy to conclude that Barbara is something of a dinosaur, part of a dying breed. But it is far from inevitable that women of this kind will form a dwindling minority. Rapid change could drive more women to hold

Back to Basics Barbara: the values of non-working women 1996

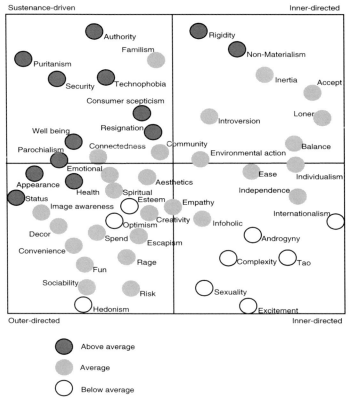

Source: *Insight '96*, Synergy Brand Values Ltd, London, 1977.

on tightly to traditional values as they conclude that feminine and family values are being squeezed out.

Pat Dade of Synergy argues that there are already signs of more women joining the Back to Basics brigade. The first group are middle-aged, rejecting independence, individualism and flexible gender roles in preference for security and traditional sources of authority. Sandwiched between the care needs of their children and the care needs of their elderly parents, they fear that the sort of supportive work that they see as their core role is no longer being valued. Some of these are the 35 to 54 year old 'Worcester women' identified by the Conservative Party as a key group of floating voters.

As well as the middle-aged, there is also a growing number of women from ethnic minority backgrounds who are more traditional in their attitudes and more family oriented: Bangladeshi and Pakistani families have 4.76 children compared to 2.4 for white families.[2]

There is also a younger group of recruits: a small but significant proportion of women who resent having to work and would rather be at home looking after the baby. Thirteen per cent of women in Synergy's survey said that they were working but would rather be at home. These women are mainly younger (primarily between 22 and 35 years old) and in social class C1.[3] Looking ahead, a period of strong economic growth might mean less pressure for both partners to work, with this group leading a return to the home.

Some of the leading examples of this set of values include Victoria Gillick, the campaigner and mother of ten children, Anne Atkins, the Daily Telegraph agony aunt, and even Paula Yates, author of a book on the virtues of women staying at home.

The family continues to top the agenda

Barbara defines herself primarily through her roles as housewife and mother. Twenty-two per cent of women in Synergy's survey agreed that 'a man's place is at work, a woman's place is in the home'. These women are more likely to be over 55 and many are in social classes D and E. They have actively chosen to maintain (or perhaps return to) traditional, family values with an emphasis on respect for authority and the promotion of a clear moral code of right and wrong. The cohort effect is clear as this chart shows.

Although *Changing lives* data shows that duty to the family has declined across the board between 1986 and 1996, it nevertheless remains high for those age groups most likely to be involved in family formation.

Many of these women feel that motherhood is insufficiently valued. They dislike the emphasis placed on work as a source of fulfilment and feel that the roles of

Family still tops the satisfaction stakes

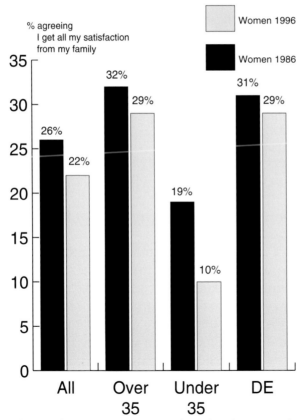

Source: *Changing lives 1986-19 96*, AGB Taylor Nelson/Future Foundation, London.

Barbara likes the old-style gender contract

Response to statement 'a husband should earn and a wife should stay at home' (%)

		Age			
		16-24	25-34	35-55	56yrs+
Agree	Women	8.4	11.1	18.1	62.9
	Men	12.5	15.7	28..5	74.4
Disagree	Women	91.6	88.9	81.9	37.1
	Men	87.5	84.3	75.5	25.6

Source: *British household panel study, Freedom's Children*, Demos, London, 1995.

housewife and full-time mother are ultimately the most rewarding. A recent survey by Grey Advertising found that 43 per cent of mothers and 31 per cent of childless women believed that they would be 'perfectly fulfilled' staying at home as wife and mother.[4] The *Changing lives* research reports similar findings, with this search for fulfilment topping the list of women's wishes in 1996. Indeed despite talk of more flexible families, 62 per cent of households with children under five are still organised along traditional lines[5] and in 2010 a large minority of mothers will still be living with a traditional gender division of labour.[6]

Work – why Barbara remains at the bottom of the ladder

Barbara is less committed to work as a source of self-esteem, and is more likely to be in low status, low paid, and frequently part-time work out of choice. In one study, 82 per cent of part-timers and 54 per cent of temporary employees were found to be women.[7] Barbara is relatively content with undemanding work. She feels little rage or frustration.[8] The educational progress of the last few decades has also had little impact on a minority of younger women who still see their role within the family as their main occupation in life and this evidence shows that the most poorly educated younger women –

especially those with fewer than four GCSEs – are still to be found in relatively unskilled and untrained work. And the closing of the pay gap that has occurred between educated young men and women has not been matched by a similar narrowing of the pay gap between young unskilled women and men.[9]

In 2010 Barbara's desire to be a good mother means that she will continue to opt for low paid, part-time work which carries fewer employment rights. The fact that this is a choice may explain why women working part time are the happiest workers of all[10] despite the widening pay gap between part-time and full-time workers and a concomitant inequality between women.[11] For Barbara, and for many other women, the 'family gap' – the gap that opens up when women have children – is becoming more significant than the pay gap between men and women.[12]

The tenacity with which many women still put family first prompted a new wave of critiques of feminism in the 1990s. Sociologist Catherine Hakim recently stoked the controversy when she described a group of the population roughly equal in size to those who compete with men (our Mannish Mels), who give priority to the 'marriage career' and prefer an undemanding job with no worries or responsibilities.[13]

Others, from inside the feminist movement, have made similar criticisms. Maureen Freely, in her book, *The mothers that feminism forgot*, argues that 'by reducing procreation to the status of a costly optional extra, the women's movement has left mothers in the lurch'.[14] Her point is indirectly supported by surveys elsewhere in Europe. These show that work and careers are not among the big factors that women cite as having changed people's lives. Instead the Pill (70 per cent), the right to vote (29 per cent) and the washing machine (28 per cent) come top.[15]

Some have pointed to another reason why family and motherhood remain important, and could become more so. This is the lack of fulfilment and progress at work, the failure to provide childcare and more balanced ways of working. If women see that, in order to achieve success, others have had to sacrifice family and ape male values, they may conclude that staying at home is a better option after all.

Less skilled women such as Barbara have in any case missed out on family-friendly policies. The business case for more flexible, woman-friendly policies, is far stronger with the highly educated. While there is still substantial unemployment, employers have little reason to be generous to the unskilled. If there is even more competition for low-skilled jobs in the future the workplace is unlikely to become any more appealing than it is today. Perhaps more women will be like Marie, a mother of thirteen quoted in the *Mail* as saying 'Motherhood is my vocation in life and it always will be'.[16]

Concerns about missing mums

Barbara disapproves of working mothers with young children. She strongly believes that family life suffers if a mother works full time. Although these views do not predominate among the younger age groups, there are more women over 55 than under and they arguably do more to set social mores. Even among younger women a significant minority – 22 per cent of 16 to 24 year olds and 36 per cent of 25 to 34 year olds – hold these values, suggesting that the Back to Basics attitudes which are

Barbara is resistant to full-time working mothers

Response to statement 'Family life suffers if mother works full time' (%)

		Age 16-24	25-34	35-55	56yrs+
Agree	Women	22.3	36.3	49.2	69.4
	Men	29.9	37.1	54.7	80.1
Disagree	Women	77.7	63.7	50.8	30.6
	Men	70.1	62.9	54.3	19.9

Source: *British household panel study, Freedom's children*, Demos, London, 1995.

held by the majority of older women (69 per cent) will not 'die out'.

In the 1990s, other forces are lending validity to Barbara's view that 'mother knows best'. Concerns are being raised about a parenting deficit[17] resulting from both parents working full time. Inadequate childcare is seen to result in unhappiness, educational under-achievement, delinquency and crime.[18] As politicians and the media play on such stories the Back to Basics lobby could come into its own. There may also be another twist: more than others, women like Barbara will be uncomfortable about the visible crisis of men. They will be more sympathetic to any calls for women to give way to men in the job market and for special programmes to help boys in schools.

In return, all that Barbara will demand is public recognition of the value of the unpaid work that she has traditionally performed. If governments offer her parenting and care allowances as compensation for staying at home, she is likely to embrace them warmly. For politicians, too, this may be attractive as a cheaper alternative to the direct provision of long term care and childcare.[19]

The prospect that the next generation of women will conclude that the promise of liberation was a false dawn may now look remote. But there are strong forces driving a pro-natalist, pro-maternal climate forward.

Well-being and health: stress hits Barbara too but perhaps less so in 2010?

Because of the low status of the domestic contribution she makes, Barbara is as prone to stress as her peers in younger more masculinised groups.[20] Research consistently shows that women who do not work are actually more likely to suffer from poor well-being than working women, even those with children who have all the stress of juggling work and home.[21]

The burden of domestic tasks is likely to continue to fall on Barbara, but since the home is her source of power and authority, she is unlikely to want to hand it over. We don't expect much change here by 2010, especially if public validation of mothering and care in the community increases. At the moment, this means that Barbara doesn't have the time or money to relax, enjoy and develop herself. And she is less likely than other women to be bothered about fitness, health, appearance and fulfilment (although *Changing lives* data shows that this is becoming less so). As this chart shows, older, poorer women are more concerned about security and money than fulfilment.

Older and poorer women are more concerned about security and money

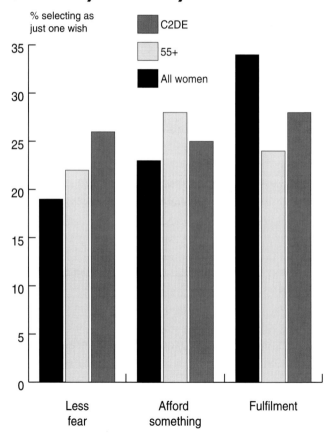

Source: *Changing lives 1996*, AGB Taylor Nelson/Future Foundation, London.

By 2010 Barbara may have overcome her technophobia. Women may welcome time-saving technological advances which make full-time housewifery a more fun and attractive option. Time saving devices such as smart tags on ready meals which will tell the microwave how they should be cooked and order a replacement from the supermarket or fleets of mouse-sized robots which will clean the carpets unaided could reduce the drudgery of housework.[22] Downloading movies on demand will keep tiring children entertained, and parents will be able to use the V chip to screen out unacceptable viewing. 'Sober up' drugs, which would allow women to down gin and tonics and pop back into sobriety when needed, could also ward off stress and boredom.

Given the spate of recent assaults in schools and anxieties about morality some mothers will want to educate their children at home.[23] In the US, home schooling has grown from 15,000 to 350,000 in ten years, as a response to concerns about the failures of the school system. For mothers at home, the need to help children with learning could be another spur to overcoming technophobia.

Will Barbara realise her power as a consumer?

Back to Basics women will wield considerable economic muscle as purchasers of goods and services, as they continue to manage the household budget. They are traditional consumers often believing that own label brands are as good as the brands promoted by advertisers. Interestingly, data from both Synergy's survey and the *Changing lives* research suggests that Barbara is a more sceptical consumer than more affluent, younger women. But there is also potential common ground with other women in demanding higher ethical standards of business. Over 60 per cent of women over 35 are very angry that companies are 'saying things that may not be true and are doing things that are probably not right'. As the chart overleaf shows, the level of anger is also higher than average among lower socio-economic groups.

Back to basics women are traditional consumers

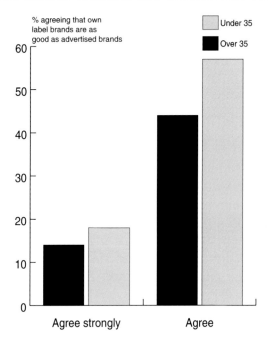

Source: *Changing lives 1996*, AGB Taylor Nelson/Future Foundation, London.

Barbara is also more cautious about believing manufacturers' promises, although she is more likely to join a retail loyalty scheme and to be loyal to branded goods than younger women. The *Changing lives* data shows that 60 per cent of women with children at home are members of a scheme compared to 23 per cent of 18 to 24 year olds.

Barbara's scepticism could become a potent force as the debate about corporate ethics and responsibility advances. Her belief in traditional moral values may make her want to see business reflect those values in products, advertising and marketing. Firms which use sex to sell products could be vulnerable to boycotts, as the Hollywood studios found in the 1990s. Equally, firms which can appeal in a modern way to C1 and C2 full-time homemakers will gain ground. Some of this thinking may explain the extraordinary shift in Ikea's strategy, exhorting women to 'chuck out the chintz' and make their homes nice, modern and bright.

Barbara is an avid mail order buyer and agent. While she is still less likely to be an early adopter of new technology (forming a large proportion of the DTI's 'nervous' and 'rejecter' technology segments)[24] she will nevertheless be happy to continue placing orders via the telephone and to use her family and local networks to generate extra income as an agent. Keener to use cash than cards, she is the least likely to use ATMs. Only 16 per cent of women over 60 and 19 per cent of women aged between 45 to 59 prefer this channel of cash withdrawal.[25]

As a traditionalist she values personal contact and may be campaigning to keep the local corner shop and library alive. She could be a loud voice for the 'humanisation' of customer service against the over-enthusiasm with which many large organisations are attempting to impose new technology such as automated call handling on the customer. Barbara does not like speaking to a computer.

Family values and politics

In politics Barbara will rally behind any cause in which families are put first and any campaign to recreate secure, stable nuclear families. She will support moves to improve public spaces and neighbourhoods, as the chart overleaf shows. Although she expects men to fill authority roles, she believes that only women can stop the rot – seeing housewives-cum-mothers like Frances Lawrence, who has called for the re-moralisation of society, as a model.

Women like Barbara provide a ready audience for the more far-reaching proposals for re-engineering the family. Michael Howard, the Home Secretary, has spoken of 'incentives and disincentives' to speed a return to the self-supporting nuclear family, ranging from American style capping on benefits for second and subsequent children of those living on welfare[26] to encouraging single pregnant women to give up their children for adoption.[27] Like Peter Lilley, the social security secretary, he wants to disadvantage women deemed to have 'behaved irresponsibly',[28] and to reform 'one of the biggest social problems of our day'.[29]

Measures of this kind go alongside the drive to move attitudes back to more traditional family values. The school has become a key battleground, with the Schools Curriculum Advisory Council recommending, after much controversy, that 'we as a society should support marriage

Generation gap: Barbara's concern for traditional values

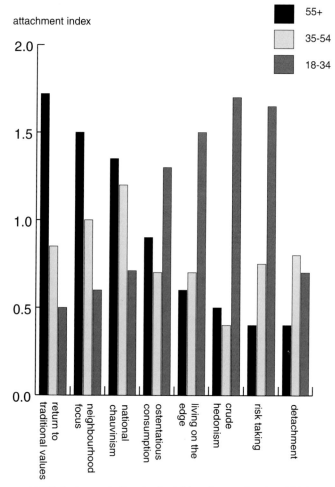

Source: MORI *Socioconsult, Freedom's children*, Demos, London, 1995.

as the traditional form of family'.[30] If social trends continue to weaken the family, we could see ever more desperate and draconian measures to shore it up. These moves would appeal to Barbara with her concern for traditional values.

But legislation is not the only area of politics relevant to women like Barbara. Community activism, long dominated by women through organisations like the Women's Institutes, could be reborn as women take up the battle for safer streets and a better environment in which to bring up their children. If public debate about the moral fabric of society becomes more intense, if evidence continues to mount about the costs of divorce and absent parents to children,[31] and if cases such as Jamie Bulger's, or Heidi Colwell's – the 'home alone' mum – continue, then women like Barbara could be mobilised to become increasingly active.

Barbara is also likely to be wary of technological advances which play with nature and biology and she may well be an active member of pro-life movements. Moral outrage against abortion – which already fuels terrorism in the United States – could also find a target in new technologies of reproduction. Women like Miss B, who decided to abort one of her twins despite having a supportive husband and living in a dual income household, induce scorn from commentators who feel there is something wrong about the abortion rate being highest among prosperous middle class mothers.[32]

World view and politics – where is the progress?

Underlying much of Barbara's world view is a romantic nostalgia for the past. She is saddened that instead of progress, the last three decades have bequeathed a nation ill at ease with itself, with family breakdown, crime and a declining sense of community. The chart opposite shows that women over 35 are three times more likely than younger women to be concerned about Britain losing moral leadership.

We expect Barbara to be strongly Euro-sceptic and

Barbara is more racist than her peers

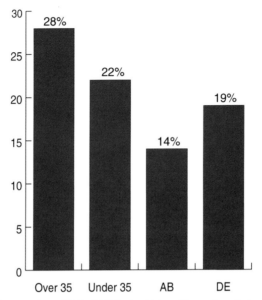

% agreeing that immigrants taking jobs are behind current unemployment

Source: *Changing lives 1996*, AGB Taylor Nelson/Future Foundation, London.

Barbara is concerned about Britain losing moral leadership in the world

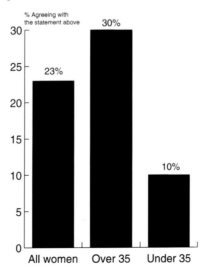

% Agreeing with the statement above

Source: *Changing lives 1996*, AGB Taylor Nelson/Future Foundation.

conservative. We already know she is more racist than her peers; women over 35, together with lower socio-economic groups, are significantly more likely to blame unemployment on immigrants and are more likely to rally behind any 'Buy British' campaign. If politicians become more comfortable presenting xenophobic views, Barbara's own attitudes could harden in tandem.

Barbara's power in the electoral marketplace

In spite of her frustration with party politics, we fully expect that in 2010 Barbara will be more likely to cast her vote than women such as Mel. Women over 55 already make up 16 per cent of the electorate, while 18 to 24 year old women make up just 6 per cent.[33] By 2010, the proportion of elderly women will have increased significantly (as the baby boomers move into old age) while the numbers of young women will have declined. For the major parties competing for votes, women like Barbara will be a key target, and social conservatism could become part of their common ground.

As parties try to bridge the gaps between different groups, we may also see more of the ambiguity that already characterises the relationships of many politicians to women voters. President Clinton, for example, has won successive presidential campaigns by appealing to working women, who rewarded him with a twenty point lead over his nearest contender each time,[34] while also presenting himself as a social conservative and mobilising mothers' votes.

Barbara's uncertain futures

At first glance Back to Basics Barbara looked like a marginal figure. But as we have seen, she could become increasingly representative and powerful in the years ahead. What then are the uncertainties?

The first big question is whether younger women really will choose full-time motherhood over other sources of fulfilment. Historical experience suggests not. When Betty Friedan wrote the *Feminine mystique* she complained of the 'problem with no name'.[35] The problem was the boredom of middle class housebound women and it became the midwife of second wave feminism with its attack on the myths of motherhood.

Younger women today may find that the service economy will allow them to work more flexibly, to achieve a balance between work and family life and to derive status and meaning from both. Material aspirations could also be critical; if women want the trappings of consumerism, they will have to be prepared to work to get them.

The investment that women make in the community could also lead to disappointment if the government washes its hands of social responsibility, and crime and social breakdown continue to worsen. Resignation could then turn to frustration and anger and to a loss of faith in the system and traditional authority.

Each of these could keep the Back to Basics brigade on the margins. But despite these caveats, the chances of women retracing their steps and returning once again to a subordinate position are not as slim as we might like to believe. At best, Barbara could wield her influence in 2010 by humanising the public sphere and raising the quality of caring and community. At worst, she could encourage a dramatic narrowing of opportunities for other women, retracing in the next century the steps taken to escape from oppression in this one.

Signs of the times

Psion 3a Series	aga
bringing in the dough	baking cookies
Vauxhall Corsa	Morris Minor
getting wired	wireless
power dressing	pretty dresses
home-shopping	home-making
changing the law	law and order
afternoon tea	sandwich generation
little old ladies	nonogenarians
satisfaction	security
patriarchs	matriarchs
microwave dinner	motherhood and apple pie
low pay	no pay
the Pill	abstinence
summer of love	sex is a chore
vigilante consumers	anti-abortion terrorists
having it all	Oxo mums
Sunday shopping	Sunday roast
B&Q	Ps and Qs
women's rights	right from wrong
Greenham Common	Worcester Woman
busy bees	busy bodies
the new parentalism	mother knows best
EMU	British bulldogs
broken families	extended families
DIY generation	whatever you say, dear
commuting	community
knocking on boardroom doors	scrubbing kitchen floors
follow the heart	hearth and home
latch key kids	learning with mother
designer labels	own brand basics
male order	mail order
NI contributions	Women's Institutes

Notes

1. *Women on the verge of the millennium*, Grey Advertising, London, 1996.

2. This is according to data from the *General household survey*, and the report, *Living in Britain, 1994*, Office of Population, Censuses and Surveys, London, 1994.

3. According to Synergy, they were clearly motivated by low levels of financial security, while at the same time being strongly committed to family values.

4. See note 1.

5. See note 2.

6. *Planning for social change, 1994-95*, The Henley Centre, London, 1995.

7. Labour force survey figures cited in: *Women's employment factsheet*, Department for Education and Employment, London, 1995.

8. Synergy's research suggests that 41 per cent of all women are not frustrated or angry.

9. Joshi H and Paci P, 1995, *Wage differentials between women and men*, Department of Employment, London. See also Harkness S and Machin S, 1995, *Changes in women's wages in Britain: what has happened to the female/male wage differential since the mid 1970s?*, Centre for Economic Performance, London School of Economics, London.

10. See for example, Curtice J, 1994, 'Satisfying work – if you can get it' in *1993-94 International social attitudes, the 10th British social attitudes report*, Social and Community Planning Research, Dartmouth Publishing, Aldershot, and also *Women: setting new priorities*, Whirlpool Foundation, Michigan, 1996.

11. See Dex S, Lissenburgh S and Taylor M, 1994, *Women and low pay: identifying the issues*, Discussion series,

Equal Opportunities Commission, Manchester, and also Barclay Sir P, 1995, *Inquiry into income and welath*, vol one, Joseph Rowntree Foundation, York. Fifty per cent of British mothers working part-time are in the three lowest occupational categories with only 10 per cent in the top three. Mouriki A, 1994, *Flexible working: towards further degradation of work, or escaping from stereotypes*, Warwick Paper in Industrial Relations, London.

12. On the family gap see: Waldfogel J, 1993, *Women working for less: a longitudinal analysis of the family gap*, discussion paper no WSP/93, Welfare State Programme, Centre for Economic Performance, London School of Economics, London, 16, and also see note 9 (Joshi and Paci, 1995). This study found that working mothers who do not take maternity leave are more likely to suffer from the family gap than women who take job protected maternity leave. On pay discrepancies between less skilled workers see note 9 (Harkness and Machin, 1995).

13. Hakim C, September 1995, 'Five feminist myths about women's employment' in *British Journal of Sociology*, vol 46, no 3.

14. Freely M, 1995, *What about us? An open letter to the mothers feminism forgot*, Bloomsbury, London.

15. 'Who loves you baby?', *The Guardian*, 9 October 1995.

16. 'Thirteen children and I'm still a size ten', *The Daily Mail*, 19 September 1996.

17. See for example, Etzioni A, 1993, *The parenting deficit*, Demos, London.

18. For a particularly controversial view of these issues see: Morgan P, 1996, *Farewell to the family? Public policy and family breakdown in Britain*

and the USA, Choice in welfare series no 21, Institute for Economic Affairs Health and Welfare Unit, London, and also Morgan P, 1996, *Who needs parents?: the effects of childcare and early education on children in Britain and the USA*, Choice in welfare series No 31, Institute for Economic Affairs Health and Welfare Unit, London. Panorama also recently stoked the flames of controversy with its programme, *Missing mum*, which reported on a two year university study which identified middle class deprivation among families where both choose to work full-time. The University of North London study of 600 families in Barking and Dagenham showed that 11 per cent of children with mothers in part-time work left school with no GCSEs. But the figure more than doubled to 25 among children whose mothers worked full-time. All the families studied had fathers in full-time work Panorama was heavily criticised for drawing national conclusions from a small survey. (See for example, 'Working mums failure blamed for children's failures', *The Guardian*, 3 February 1997.)

19. See Wilkinson H, 1994, *No turning back: generations and the genderquake*, Demos, London, and Wilkinson H and Mulgan G, 1995, *Freedom's children: work,relationships and politics for 18-34 years olds in Britain today*, Demos, London.

20. Sixty-eight per cent of women aged between 45 and 59 agree that they often or sometimes suffer from stress nowadays, compared with 66 per cent of 25 to 44 year olds and 65 per cent of 16 to 24 year olds. *Planning for social change 1994-95*, The Henley Centre, London, 1995.

21. See note 19 (Wilkinson and Mulgan, 1995). This study analysing data from the British Household Panel Study clearly showed that people in work at all ages are strikingly happier than those out of work. And in every age group, working women – even if they have children – are happier than women who are at home.

22. 'Supper to cook?, Clothes to wash? Just leave it to the tag', *The Observer*, 29 December 1996. For further information about the details of the innovations mentioned here, how they are likely to work and when they could come on line see: Pescovitz D and Wieners B, 1996, *Reality check*, Hardwired books, San Francisco.

23. Interactive lessons, classroom conferencing and the electronic filing of homework are all functions of the Net which could be coordinated to facilitate the virtual school/university should the will be put behind the project. Large class sizes could be countered by electronically personalised lessons and parents could overcome geographical boundaries to enrol their children at their preferred school.

24. *IT for all*, Department of Trade and Industry, London, 1996.

25. See note 20 (The Henley Centre, 1995).

26. 'Howard seeks curb on child benefit to boost morality', *The Daily Telegraph*, 6 October 1996.

27. 'Give up your baby plan for lone mothers', *The Sunday Telegraph*, 10 October 1993.

28. 'Support for challenge to maternity proposals', *The Daily Telegraph*, 29 September 1993.

29. 'Ministers ride out storm on lone parents', *The Daily Telegraph*, 10 November 1993.

30. 'New code for children will snub values of the family', *The Mail on Sunday*, 22 September 1996 and 'Moral guideline for schools says marriage is best', *The Independent*, 20 December 1996.

31. See Cockett M and Tripp J, 1994, *Children living in reordered families*, Social policy research findings 45, Joseph Rowntree Foundation, York. See also Dennis N and Erdos G, 1992, *Families without fatherhood*, Institute for Economic Affairs, London, and also Kraemer S, 1995, *Active fathering for the future*, Demos, London.

32. See for example, 'Would you put one of them down too?', *The Daily Mail*, 7 August 1996. This article also claimed that aborting the twins was analagous to anaesthetising one of two elderly parents because you could not take the stress of accommodating them. Likening scientific progress to uncorking 'a genie that can never be put back in the bottle', the editorial view is over-ridingly one of technology being out of control. Miss B was also offered donations of thousands of pounds from anti-abortion charities to keep the baby.

33. Stephenson M A, 1996, *Winning women's votes*, Fawcett Society, London.

34. Diplock S and Wilkinson H, 1996, *Soft sell or hard policies: how can the parties best appeal to women?*, Demos, London.

35. Friedan B, 1963, *The feminine mystique*, Gollancz, London.

Explosion or implosion: Frustrated Fran

Frustrated Fran has grown up believing that feminism should by now be delivering results: her pay should be equal to that of her male counterparts, her partner should take an equal share of domestic responsibilities and childcare, work should be the source of success, creativity and fulfilment, and good quality childcare should be available on demand. But reality has failed to keep up with her expectations. She feels she is expected to act like a superwoman, effortlessly juggling jobs, home and motherhood, but lacks the support she needs to be able to cope, let alone to realise her full potential.

The Frustrated Frans are relatively young – under 35 – and in the social groups C1, C2 and D. Many are also single parents. Their jobs are typically unskilled, part-time and on fixed-term contracts, and they give little in the way of either fulfilment or financial reward. According to Synergy's survey, a solid 15 per cent of all women feel they are getting a raw deal out of life and we estimate that some 33 per cent of all women share many of Fran's frustrations.[1] Amongst this group, many are mothers with young children who feel hemmed in by the lack of state support, the absence of affordable childcare and the unhelpful attitudes of their male partners.[2]

Frustrated Fran

Others are older women whose children have flown the nest and who, in their fifties, want to take the opportunities they missed when they were young.[3] Both groups have been influenced by feminism, but lack either the qualifications or the money to easily realise their dreams.

Carol Jackson in EastEnders, who juggles two part-time jobs and looks after four children, is a good example for whom the strain of keeping afloat puts pressure on her relationships with both her partner and her children.

The evidence suggests that women like Fran are getting angry, and growing in number. Twenty-three per cent of all women report that they feel angry much of the time – most of them under 25 and in socio-economic groups D and E, women who have absorbed some feminist values but feel disempowered in a consumer society. Unemployed women are the angriest of all,[4] and that includes many second generation 16 to 24 year old ethnic minority women, black and Pakistani in particular, who are suffering worse unemployment than their male equivalents (reversing the picture amongst young white people). If the pressures on the labour market continue, this group will grow.

In contrast to Mel who senses that her time has come, Naomi who is networking to make it happen and Angela who has the luxury of being able to make a choice, Fran feels cut out of the action, and lacks confidence in herself. Thirty-one per cent of all women in Synergy's survey say they suffer from poor self-esteem, and 27 per cent feel resigned rather than optimistic. Rather than being supported by her 'sisters' she finds herself increasingly marginalised by the successes of Mannish Mel who has the education, support and determination to succeed. By 2010 some of the resulting anger could be ready to explode. Already demonstrating a mix of pessimism, escapism and rage, Fran is as likely to turn on women as on men, with the girl gangs of the 1990s possible harbingers of things to come (see chart overleaf).

Frustrated Fran 1996

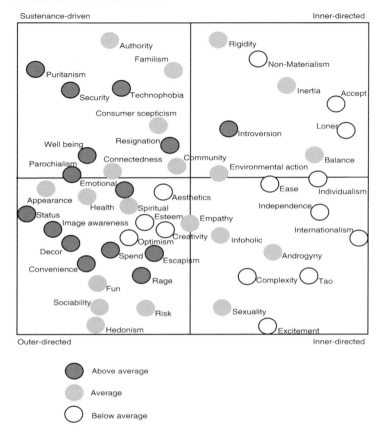

Source: *Insight '96*, Synergy Brand Values Ltd, London, 1977.

Fran's dilemma is neatly encapsulated by the film *Thelma and Louise*,[5] which portrays disempowered women who are liberated by a combination of escape and revenge after the experience of rape, but in the end have nowhere to go. Other celluloid examples include *Shirley Valentine* and a less well known film, *Accidental meeting*,[6] in which a woman driven mad by her materialistic husband's infidelity, murders the oppressive boss of a chance acquaintance she has met, under the impression that she is committing a just act.

Frustration has long been a key issue for modern women. Elaine Showalter has written about the similarities between the symptoms of hysteria, which were explained by male doctors in a variety of implausible ways, and shell-shock in soldiers, the result of being in a constricted space, with little control over one's destiny.[7] The earlier manifestations of women's frustration provided much of the material for the psychoanalytic movement. Freud's earliest clients were classic hysterics who were unable to move their bodies due to the frustration and abuse they suffered. In the 1950s and 1960s it was the frustration of women consigned to the 'suburban habitat' and artificial isolation that provided the spark for the second wave of feminism.

However, what is different now is that frustration is mounting not as the fuel for feminism, but rather as a consequence of it. The success of other women enables them to see more precisely just how they are being failed. What is less clear is whether Fran and her sisters will get angry enough to revitalise the feminist revolution, and inject a harder edged egalitarian politics or whether their anger will remain primarily private and directed inwards.

Great expectations and slow-moving reality

Fran's sense of self

Fran is seeking autonomy, albeit within clear boundaries. She is more likely than Back to Basics Barbara to resist traditional gender roles and may well be experimenting with different roles, especially if she is working. But unlike Mannish Mel she lacks confidence that her aspirations will be realised. For her, more than for her mother's generation, meaning comes not just from childcare and homemaking but also increasingly from life outside the family, from hobbies, sport and exercise, and from work.

The Frustrated Frans would like to be valued for themselves and would like to be able to explore their identities, relishing any opportunity to release the 'wild woman within'.[8] Yet lack of self-confidence means they are still highly dependent on validation from their family, partner, work colleagues and boss. According to Synergy's survey, 11 per cent of women worry a great deal about what others think of them.

Fran's family and relationships
In her older incarnation, Fran has probably accepted second best when it comes to the man in her life. In her younger incarnations she is generally hoping that he will take more responsibility for things, but she is liable to be disappointed. A recent study by Demos found that while 69 per cent of 18 to 34 year olds thought that men and women should do equal shares of domestic work, the reality was quite different: in 77 per cent of cases women did most of the cooking, in 66 per cent of cases they did most of the shopping, in 75 per cent of cases they did most of the cleaning, and in 85 per cent most of the laundry.[9]

Family life is still important to Fran even if, like most women, she will probably have fewer children, later than her mother's generation (the average age of women at the birth of their first child has risen from 23.5 in 1970 to 26.2 in 1993).[10] Her family comes first but, unlike previous generations, and unlike more traditional contemporaries, she would like to be able to renegotiate the terms of her commitments – not so as to spend less time with the children, but rather to leave her more space to follow her own interests. In practice, however, low pay and skills mean that she is not only unlikely to be able to manage this; she is also liable to even more stress than her high flying contemporaries.

Changing lives data shows that although since 1986 women as a whole have come to seek less satisfaction from family life, one quarter of C2D women still seek most satisfaction coming from the family – reflecting the inadequacies of the workplace that does no more than provide an income – compared to just over 20 per cent amongst C1 women and less than 15 per cent of AB.

Traditionally, responsibility for caring for the young, elderly and frail has rested with women. Fran is unlikely either to relish this role or to be able to afford to buy in

Frustrated Fran is still most likely to get satisfaction from her family

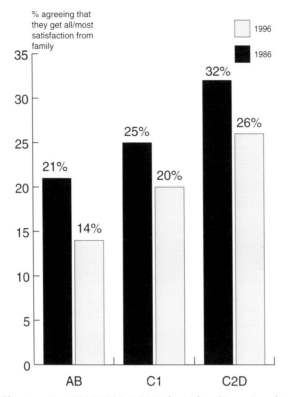

% agreeing that they get all/most satisfaction from family

☐ 1996
■ 1986

Source: *Changing Lives 1986-1996*, AGB Taylor Nelson/Future Foundation, London.

help. A steadily ageing population will probably mean more pressures falling on women like her, particularly if the state tries to withdraw from care. Already, women aged between 35 and 54 are more likely to be in work than ever before. In 1971, 62 per cent of women aged between 35 and 54 were economically active. In 1994 this figure had increased to 75 per cent and it is predicted to be as high as 81 per cent in 2006.[11] Most of these women have families and, although better qualified than women over 55 years old, they are still relatively unqualified, and many are in fairly low skill, repetitive jobs. Whereas wealthy women may spend ever more of their income on both childcare and eldercare, this will not be an option

147

for women on low incomes. Fran and her sisters could find that, instead of being liberated and independent, they have become the 'sandwich generation', caring for both parents and children at the same time. Nor is technology likely to be a solution, since most of the time-saving technologies are likely to be expensive and Fran is more technophobic than average.

Work – why doesn't Fran realise her potential?

Fran wants work to be a source of meaning as well as economic independence, even if it doesn't result in a career. This dual view of work was clearly articulated by one young Asian woman factory worker in a recent Demos study:

> Sometimes you don't like work but you have to come for the money. When I had maternity leave for a while I

Fran's frustrated ambition

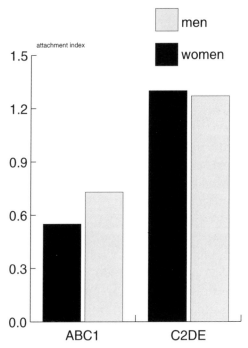

Source: MORI *Socioconsult, Freedom's children*, Demos, London, 1995.

ended up getting bored. I really wanted to go to work. Even though it's not really a career. I enjoy the job.[12]

But at work, Fran is clearly frustrated. While younger women, especially among socio-economic groups C1 and C2 have become increasingly oriented towards success, Demos' research shows they feel their ambitions are being frustrated.

There is a gap between expectations and reality. A survey by the Whirlpool Foundation found that British working women (44 per cent) are more concerned than in the other four European countries surveyed about organisations not valuing the people who work for them, and another survey found that 37 per cent of full-time working mothers felt that they had skills which were not being applied at work.[13] The pay gap between men and women both reflects and reinforces a culture in which their work is less valued than men's. This problem is more acute among low-skilled women than professionals. Just as at home technology is not much of a help, so too at work Fran is more likely to see new technologies as threats to jobs rather than liberators.

The frustrations with work are also heightened by inflexibility. Many working women want flexible working hours but there is a mismatch between the desire for flexible work and what is actually on offer.

The combination of global trends and government policies has also contributed to a less secure labour market and has dampened many working women's expectations. According to data from *Changing lives*, women who work full time are opting more for security rather than excitement at work. Sixty-one per cent of full-time working women made this choice in 1996, an increase of 19 per cent over the 1986 figure. And precisely because labour market forecasters predict that there will still be many routine, boring, unskilled and low paid jobs in 2010 – perhaps even more than today as jobs are created in fields like care and domestic services – it is understandable that the women for whom this work is the only option will not be inspired by career opportunities. Thus, instead of boosting self-esteem, work becomes a burden, a force for deepening resignation and pessimism. The glass ceiling is not even an issue for Fran – she is far from even being able to bang her head on it.

Fran seeks an escape in hedonism and consumption

Outside work, women like Fran enjoy spending and consuming for their own sakes.[14] They are status oriented and outer directed and clearly enjoy spending money, especially on home decor. Consumption is a way of asserting individuality; it is a source of power as well as being fun. Work all too often reinforces powerlessness.

Materialism wins over fulfilment

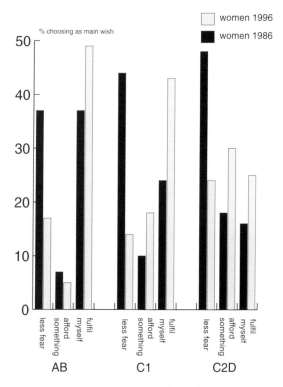

Source: *Changing Lives 1986-1996*, AGB Taylor Nelson/Future Foundation,

Changing lives data shows that over the last decade the lower socioeconomic groups (C2Ds) have remained most attached to material fulfilment at 30 per cent of the total, as opposed to the self-fulfilment that is now first choice among the most affluent.

Consumption is one area where technology is set to play an important role, with the use of time saving devices such as the self-scanning of grocery shopping which is now available in Safeway stores to cut out queues. Smart card technologies which can record an individual's most regular purchases and have them automatically delivered are also set to become more prevalent. Added convenience and value will be important to this group, as will higher moral standards in business.

Fran at play

Women like Fran share many of the values of their generation, including such masculine values as hedonism, the desire for success and the willingness to take risks. Fran in this sense is similar to Mannish Mel but with one key difference: where Mel is optimistic, Fran is pessimistic about her fate.

Resignation is also matched by the desire for escapism and risk as well as hedonism, fun and sociability. Lack of money means, however, that it is harder to realise this goal in healthy ways. Instead, anger and frustration tend to fuel the growing use of alcohol and cigarettes among less affluent women.

Fran's politics

Women like Fran are unlikely to be involved in politics. They care about a wide range of issues but feel their views are not taken into account. Not surprisingly, *Changing lives* data shows they are far more likely to support trade unions than other groups, reflecting their occupational status and their experience of powerlessness at work. In 1996, 27 per cent of C2D women accepted the authority of trade unions compared with only 15 per cent of AB women.

Fran looks to trade unions

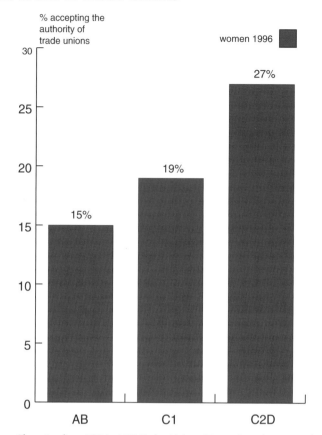

% accepting the
authority of
trade unions

women 1996

Source: *Changing lives 1996*, AGB Taylor Nelson/Future Foundation, London.

Although they may get involved locally, mobilising around specific issues, such as safety, schools or air pollution, they haven't yet found a way of expressing their frustration.

However, although this group is distrustful of traditional political parties, they are more likely to vote for a party which values women's role and equal opportunities, They do not see themselves as feminists. For them feminism is something created by and benefiting more affluent women like Mannish Mel. The largely middle class rhetoric of feminism fails to resonate with the reality of their lives and those from ethnic minority groups may feel unable to identify with the overwhelmingly white, higher educated tone of the movement.[15] They are more likely to blame their frustrations and insecurity on external forces and other people. *Changing lives* data shows they are twice as likely to blame immigrants for taking jobs and six times as likely to blame excessive wage claims for unemployment.

In their world view they are parochial and communitarian rather than internationalist. *Changing lives* data confirms they are less aware of the effects of global competition and new technology than richer women. They are likely to view foreign travel as an exciting,

Frustrations are more likely to be blamed on external forces

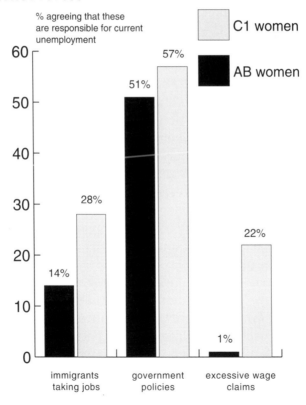

Source: *Changing lives 1996*, AGB Taylor Nelson/Future Foundation, London.

hedonistic pursuit and something to aspire to, although their real opportunities to travel may be limited. Yet in spite of their parochialism, some identify with media images of women in other countries who face similar frustrations.

Frustrated Fran's uncertain futures

Fran is torn between a desire to escape her current situation and the fact that she has little chance to do so. What then are the uncertainties?

From frustration to change?
The first possibility is that women like Fran will respond actively to the obstacles in their way. Instead of resenting more successful women, they will identify with them; 17 per cent of women in Synergy's survey agreed that they don't get mad, they get even. The numbers saying this are likely to have increased considerably by 2010. Thus far most of the women moving into self-employment or entrepreneurship have been professionals, but by 2010, with continuing high levels of unemployment and the growing demand for personal services such as domestics, home health care and childcare, many smaller, more localised businesses may have been set up by less qualified women frustrated at waiting for opportunities in the mainstream. In the United States, the fastest growing job categories include home health aides and nurses, and these may create big opportunities for this group, often working for the more successful, 'time squeezed' professionals. Out of this work, a series of new networks could arise, financed both by the public sector and through market demand, and catering to the special needs of ethnic minority communities, single parents and working women. Such might be a possible base for a revived feminist movement, which would then be able to use the political system to win concessions on issues such as childcare, flexible working and welfare.

Explosive frustration: a threat to social cohesion
The second possibility is that women like Fran will reject their traditional roles. Many will be home alone mums, others will refuse to care for the elderly, still more will leave their husbands. Frustration will lead to rage and revolt, a 'second genderquake'. The heroines of such a revolt might include figures such as Lorena Bobbitt, the American woman who severed her abusive husband's penis, and the British woman who cut one arm off all of her unfaithful husband's designer suits and delivered his vintage wine to the neighbours with their milk.

As women become increasingly masculine in their values – hedonistic, risk-taking and even aggressive, their failure to achieve a proper stake in the economy could turn them towards an increasingly anti-social and alienated lifestyle. In practice, however, it is likely that most of the anger would end up being directed against their own communities and those closest to them – like today's teenage 'underwolves'.[16] Whether the anger could become sufficiently focused and well-organised to achieve change is less clear.

Women in the ghetto
The most depressing, and for a significant minority, the most likely future is one in which women simply turn their frustration inwards. Thirteen per cent of women in Synergy's survey strongly agree that there is no use trying because it won't make any difference. These women are resigned to their fate and are more traditional in their values, sharing many of the prejudices and aspirations of Back to Basics Barbara. But instead of becoming angry, they become depressed or seek ways to dull the pain through drink or drugs – a response to their lack of opportunities. It is significant that the 27 per cent of women who are pessimistic are also introverted and increasingly inert, while the 16 per cent of women in our sample who are in socio-economic group D combine resignation and escapism. The growing use of drugs such as Prozac, Temazepam and Valium shows how much

155

social problems have now come to be dealt with as if they were personal ones. One journalist who interviewed Elizabeth Wurtzel, author of the best-selling novel *Prozac nation* wrote:

> When patients visit their doctor with symptoms of depression they are prescribed Prozac within three minutes of describing their symptoms.[17]

In addition to depression, frustration manifests itself in such disorders as anorexia and bulimia, which are both associated with a desire to take control of one's life, and self-harm, where the anger a person feels towards external situations is misdirected in shockingly physical ways. Already, an estimated 5 to 10 per cent of young American women are anorexic, while up to six times this number are bulimic. While this has been a predominantly middle class phenomenon, there is now evidence that eating disorders are increasingly common among lower income groups.[18] If the causes of frustration are left unattended, by 2010 Britain could have a large minority of women going to any lengths to blot out reality.

We expect the Frustrated Frans to make up a significant minority by 2010. Unless current trends in the labour market change significantly, there will be more frustration and more anger. But the weight of this group in society will be masked by their relative lack of power and influence. In politics, as at home and in work, their fate is to be taken for granted, not attended to.

Signs of the times

hemming curtains	hemmed in
juggling	nervous breakdown
24hr office	working round the clock
Wonder bra	lack of support
step machine	treadmill existence
Amy Johnson	Shirley Valentine
looking back in anger	explosive frustration
going into labour	labour force
smashing glass ceiling	gazing up at glass ceiling
great expectations	reality bites
identity crisis	confidence crisis
sisters doing it for themselves	I can't get no satisfaction
penis envy	Bobitting
the Pill	Prozac
autonomy	monotony
oppression	depression
emancipation	emaciation
Argos	Ikea
high flying	tumble drying
aspiration	frustration
women's work	women's work
no work	overwork
career	job
getting even	getting mad
coffee mornings	sandwich generation
new man	no man
the great escape	cigarettes and alcohol
parents	single parent

Notes

1. These women are in search of convenience products, and seek an outlet for their rage, resignation, and consumer scepticism in escapism.

2. See *Releasing the woman within*, Ogilvy and Mather, London, 1994.

3. See for example, Sheehy G, 1996, *New passages*, HarperCollins, London. She argues that this pattern is especially common among middle class women. However, our research would suggest that this is increasingly the case among lower socio-economic groups.

4. These women are seeking an escape from their current situation. They are attracted to anything that brings some excitement into their life. They are independent and reject Britishness.

5. *Thelma and Louise*, 1991, Ridley Scott, dir.

6. *Accidental meeting*, 1993, Michael Zinberg, dir.

7. See Showalter E, 1987 in Higonnet MR, ed, *Behind the Lines*, Yale University Press, New Haven, Connecticut.

8. See note 2.

9. Wilkinson H and Mulgan G, *Freedom's children: work, relationships and politics for 18-34 year olds in Britain today*, Demos, London.

10. *Social focus on women*, Central Statistical Office, London, 1995.

11. Department of Employment figures cited in 'Is the future female?' in *Planning for Social Change 1996-1997*, Henley Centre, London, 1997.

12. Wilkinson H, 1995, *Through the eyes of the shop-floor worker*, Seven Million Project working paper 12, Demos, London.

13. *Women: setting new priorities*, Whirlpool Foundation, Benton Harbor, Michigan, 1996.

14. Synergy's survey suggests that the 23 per cent of women who feel angry seek status and are image conscious. They enjoy spending money, especially on decoration and convenience products. These women are sociable and are seeking fun. Hedonistic in their behaviour, they are also more inclined to take risks.

15. Siann G and Wilkinson H, 1995, *Gender, feminism and the future*, Demos, London.

16. See note 8, 17. This book drew on a survey by MORI Socioconsult which reported that 'Over half of under 25 year olds register as profoundly disconnected from the system, and a growing number of "underdogs" are now prepared to bite back. We call them "underwolves".'

17. 'Young and hyped in America', *The Independent*, 17 May 1995.

18. See Wolf N, 1990, *The beauty myth*, Chatto and Windus, London.

The forward march of women halted?

I wanna do great things,
Don't wanna compromise
I wanna know what life is
I wanna try everything...[1]
– *Echobelly*

We have described five of tomorrow's women and suggested some of the forces that are set to shape their lives and attitudes. In this concluding chapter we pull the themes together. We describe the issues that are likely to concern women in 2010 and we ask how successful women will be in promoting them.

Who will predominate?
We don't pretend to be able to predict which of the five types of woman will predominate in 2010. If current trends continue, postmaterial and new age values look most likely to strengthen, becoming the natural successors to the consumerism of the 1980s and 1990s.

Linear forecasts also give grounds for expecting the 'future is female' scenario to be realised. The trends towards a 'feminising' of the workplace, the convergence of young men's and women's values, greater control over reproduction and even male infertility, all point to a future where feminine values will continue to displace masculine ones.

But as we have seen there are many reasons for doubting the linear extrapolation from current trends. We have uncovered important ways in which the current situation for women is unstable:

● Women's continuing move into the workplace has occurred without any corresponding change in the frameworks for time, leave and welfare – making Britain very different from other countries, like those in Scandinavia, where women have a relatively equal place at work.

● Work has not been adequately adapted to the needs of the family and parenting. Here, too, Britain has been far behind other countries, and the effect of the failure to keep institutions up to speed with social changes has been to place a heavier burden on women, who are as a result working harder, and suffering greater stress than elsewhere.

● The growing 'crisis of masculinity' has left a minority of men, particularly in the north, pessimistic about their chances, performing badly at school and failing to get into jobs when they leave school. Looking ahead this could either give a further boost to women's confidence at home and at work or it could prompt governments to adopt special measures to help men in a direct inversion of positive action policies for women.

We have already pointed to some of the likely effects of these instabilities. Some women will adopt more masculine values to ensure that they can succeed at work. Others will continue to be frustrated and angry. Meanwhile pressures on the family will encourage currents of social conservatism, which are already being swelled by what are seen to be worsening problems of social order.

The most likely outcome, of course, is not that one type of woman will come to predominate. Instead the diversity of economic, demographic and technological pressures makes it more likely that there will be a further fracturing of values and experiences. But we can nevertheless identify some of the big issues that will be high on the agenda of tomorrow's women.

An agenda for 2010 – twelve big issues for tomorrow's women

1. Achieving balance

For most women achieving a better balance between family and work is more important than it was ten years ago. The priorities include: reducing working time, providing support to make sure that childbearing and work are genuinely rather than theoretically compatible, lengthening school hours and organising more activities for children outside the home, and recognising the importance of personal fulfillment across a number of fronts to achieve well-being. Parental leave will be a key issue, with important arguments to be resolved about how it is to be paid for and how it can be matched to the needs of small firms that will employ 50 per cent of the private sector workforce. Policies that help women to achieve balance will be supported by a very wide range of groups - from traditionalists to women wanting careers.

2. Harnessing technology

Women are in danger of falling behind technologically and they are not doing enough to shape the development of new technologies to their own needs. Women will need to become more involved in debates about use of information technology by girls in schools and at home, the delivery of public services, the availability of tools for easing the combination of work and home. The EU concept of a driving licence for computers has some merit – providing it is popularised and the necessary training and experience are made available to women.

3. Maximising the childbearing window

There may be strong arguments for making it easier for women to have children earlier – at the moment all of the incentives push the opposite way. The fact that women are having children later is primarily an effect of inflexibility at work – but it potentially causes problems for health, leading to complications and added costs. Women should feel free to choose when to have children.

4. Giving more value to care

Women will remain the majority of care workers and they will be particularly affected by policies on long term care, not only because they live longer than men but also because they are the main carers, whether paid or unpaid. For them, it will be preferable for tax-financed or insurance-financed long term care schemes to generate paid work for women carers rather than depending on informal care. They will want to see governments give a greater value to caring work. Fiscally strapped governments by contrast, will try to resist.

5. Insuring against changing risks and flexible lives

Women need new forms of insurance, for example to insure against illness of children or partners forcing them to stay at home; to prepare for maternity breaks or parental leave; or to prepare for divorce, which is often a severe financial shock, and still leaves women much worse off. There is also a more general need for better ways to manage varying activities through the life cycle, making it easier to take up education at different life stages, and to move between work, parenting and learning.

6. Matching time-rich and time-poor to provide services

Given the time squeeze on the working population, harnessing the energy of the time-rich (unemployed, older people and mothers with older children) could be critical to many women's quality of life. There should be a common interest in encouraging working women to buy more services from currently unemployed women.

7. *Making public spaces women-friendly*
Women are still inadequately considered when buildings and public spaces are designed. We anticipate that the combination of greater assertiveness by women and greater concerns for safety will lead to more women-centred policies for city design, ranging from women-only car parks, to new ways of ensuring public spaces are full of activity, and from a renewed interest in buses, which are mainly used by women, to better lighting policies.

8. *Activity beyond jobs*
With rising life expectancy many women have much more time than ever before. Many older women, like older men, become relatively inactive, even when they are still fit and healthy. We predict much more energy going into ways to mobilise older women as active citizens, in everything from volunteering and mentoring, to 'grans' armies' helping with childcare.[2] Success in doing this could be a crucial ingredient in reducing the stresses on younger women with children.

9. *Supporting women entrepreneurs*
Most programmes of support for business still have in mind a male entrepreneur. In the future there will be more demand for programmes overtly targetted to women, through advice, training and support networks organised out of Business Links. Women may increasingly fight to take over local business organisations - like Chambers of Commerce - which remain dominated by men.

10. *Training and skills for parents*
Although women do well in formal education they fall behind in terms of training, mainly because of more discontinuous patterns of work. Any legal requirements on employers to provide training more equitably (at the

moment the great majority of spending goes on the already qualified) will benefit women. We should expect more demands for training entitlements to follow periods of time off for parenting, as crucial ways of closing pay and opportunity gaps that accompany starting a family.

11. Empowering women as comsumers

Women are not only the main consumers of commercial products and services, they are also the main users of public services. Policies which provide more information, more choice and better quality of service will benefit women. Smart card technology, properly conceived, could serve as an effective citizens' empowerment device in 'consumerising' many services provided by central government, as well as putting advanced technology into the hands of all citizens in a form with which they will be familiar.

12. Healthier living

Women are already more aware of their health than men. Values changes are likely to make them even more conscious about health risks. But at the same time their lifestyles are becoming less healthy, with rising stress, smoking and alcohol consumption. New approaches to providing health services more holistically, at home and at work, will become increasingly important, particularly if the life expectancy gap between men and women begins to narrow, as many forecast.

Common interests?

What is interesting about this list is that, although there remain major differences of interest and values between women, and although these differences may grow in the years ahead, there are large areas of common interest. While women will be divided over issues such as abortion and tax cuts, or over the styles of organisations and politics, they will tend to agree on many of these issues. Traditionalists and progressives are coming to share a good deal of common ground on achieving better balance between work and family. Old and young share a common interest in finding new ways to mobilise the elderly as volunteers. All women share a common interest in shaping public institutions and public spaces to fit women's needs better.

Using power

If they can reach agreement, what means will women have to put these issues at the top of the public agenda? Much depends on where women devote their energies and on what they see as their own priorities. The chart below provides a way of thinking about this.

Over the last decade most of women's energy has been directed to the right hand side of the diagram. Women have been concentrating on the personal – on health, fitness, lifestyle and increasing their earning power. Little has been done to change the work environment – partly because of the weakness of work-based organisations, and women have failed to use their muscle as consumers to change other women's lives. However, for all the reasons we have set out, there is a good chance that women will

Where will women direct their energies?

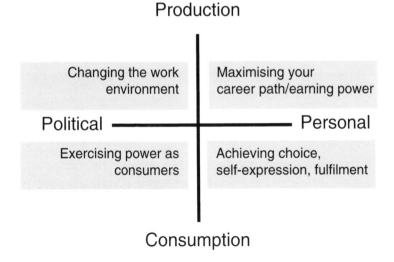

Production

Changing the work environment | Maximising your career path/earning power

Political — Personal

Exercising power as consumers | Achieving choice, self-expression, fulfilment

Consumption

move from the bottom right hand quadrant of the chart towards the left, as a response to the barriers they are now encountering at work and in society at large. As they do so we may see the maturing of a range of new 'feminisms' – business feminism, consumer feminism, and new movements of 'remoralisation' led by women.

Consumer activism?

There have been some striking successes of consumer activism – like the campaigns across Europe to stop Shell disposing of the Brent Spar rig in the North Sea. Oxfam have introduced the concept of 'serious shopping' in an attempt to raise consumer awareness and change shopping habits.[3] Campaigns on trade have also had an impact. But despite women's significance as consumers, there has been remarkably little effort to mobilise women to punish companies which treat female employees badly, or which provide women with unsatisfactory consumer goods. The Women's Environmental Network provides a telephone information line for checking products, but more initiatives have come from companies – like the latest Body Shop initiative *Body and Soul*, a free magazine arguing for liberation from the idealised images presented in the media, and a re-birth of self esteem[4] – than from campaigning organisations. However, as women become more familiar with being politicised consumers, it might not be too long before there are kitemarks for companies that are ahead of the game on family-friendly policies.

What about the workplace?

The equal opportunities legislation in the United States and here initially led to a series of high profile cases and strikes (such as the women machinists strike at Ford in 1978). Ever since there have been many, albeit small scale, campaigns by groups of women employees trying to improve their position at work. However, few of these have been either very successful or very influential, partly because the main vehicles for change – the trade unions – have not been seen as sympathetic to women. This could be changing and, looking ahead, we could see more assertive action by women to bring issues such as childcare, leave policies and time into the bargaining process. Much will probably depend on the wider economic environment. Against a backdrop of unemployment, low skilled women will not dare to risk their jobs by taking action. However, if unemployment continues to fall the climate will change, as it did in the late 1980s when pressures of demand in some parts of the labour market made employers much more keen to attract women.

What about politics?
Earlier generations of feminists believed that women's shared interests outweighed their differences. They hoped that it would make sense for women to campaign together – perhaps even with their own political parties. Around some issues, such as pay and parenting, there are clearly shared interests, and most of the policy issues described in the previous section are relevant to the majority of women. But to hold a political movement together it would be necessary for women's values to be much more homogeneous than they are. On some issues – such as those involving the balance between work and home – fathers and mothers probably share more in common than mothers and single women. We consider it unlikely that women will combine together in shared political movements.

But it doesn't follow that the depoliticised 'post-feminism' of the 1990s will continue in its present form. Many older women will have more time available and many others will benefit from the confidence that comes with being better educated. Given the gaps that we have identified between expectations and reality, the next few years could bring a range of new forms of activism, from the moral crusades of older traditionalist women to strikes by frustrated women at the workplace fighting for better treatment. A decade ago many wrongly forecast that by the late 1990s nationalism would be a thing of the past. Similarly, too, it would be unwise to forecast that feminism will become a solely individual matter.

Toolboxes for tomorrow's women

Whether as employees, consumers or citizens, women's capacity to achieve change will depend on their access to the relevant tools. As we have seen, there are widely varying degrees of access to technology, money and skills, and the differences are more likely to widen than to contract. In some cases the patterns of access will be shaped by changes in the labour market. In other cases public policies will be crucial. But the table below provides a useful benchmark for judging how far women progress, and how much they gain control over the means to determine their own lives.

Toolboxes

TOOLS OF EMPOWERMENT

○ Access to technology

○ Wealth creation

○ Education/skills development

○ Participation/contribution to local community

TOOLS OF CHOICE

○ 'Leave' accounts and credits

○ Supportive family structures

○ Continuous education

○ Parental leave arangements

TOOLS OF WELL-BEING

○ Health education

○ Well woman services

○ Consumer choice of provision

○ Reproductive choice

TOOLS OF COMMUNITY

○ Safe communal spaces

○ Participation in social capital creation

○ New networks/supports

○ Benefit from programmes

Where next?

The last few decades have brought a more profound revolution in women's lives than any other period in human history. Women have become voters, workers and leaders. They have come to take for granted their right to share in power and opportunity, and a younger generation is now more confident than ever.

So deep has been the shift in values that there is little prospect of this historical tide going into reverse. There are still many traditionalists. And there are many women who are uncertain about the future. But their weight in the polity and in culture is too limited to turn the clock back decisively.

As this report has shown, however, there is a danger that the forward march could come to a halt or dissipate. If women's expectations are not met; if new opportunities are not matched by policies to enable women to balance careers and family; if the barriers to less skilled women are not overcome, then we should expect to see rising anger and resentment.

In many respects the new century brings another set of extraordinary opportunities. Just as the pill liberated women in the 20th century so will many new technologies liberate women to better manage their lives and control their reproductive capacities. Within work, the shift to an information and service based economy will mean a continuing expansion of opportunities. In leisure women will be able to explore themselves in new ways, to travel, to take risks and have fun.

But realising all of these opportunities will demand some concerted action: to achieve flexibility in time; to properly value care. And since 51 per cent of women, however different their values and beliefs, still define their self-identity through being a parent, the task of redefining parenting to fit a very different, and more egalitarian culture will be the most critical challenge of all⊙

Notes

1. Echobelly, 1995, *Pantyhose and roses*, Rhythmn King, London.

2. 'Granny's army', *The Guardian*, 29 January 1997.

3. 'Oxfam encourages high street on exploitation', *The Independent*, 20 May 1996.

4. *The body and self esteem*, The Body Shop, Littlehampton, 1997.

Appendix: methodologies

The Future Foundation

The *Changing lives* data presented in this report is from new research by the Future Foundation and AGB Taylor Nelson. The information was obtained as part of RSGB's General Omnibus Surveys for October 1996. The survey was based on a representative sample of 1,000 adults, males and females aged sixteen or older. They were selected in a minimum of 130 sampling points. Respondents were interviewed at home by interviewers between 9 and 13 October 1996. The 1986 data was obtained through the same process and is directly comparable, allowing us to consider how attitudes and values have changed over time.

Synergy Brand Values Ltd

Synergy Brand Values Ltd is a consultancy which analyses the impact of dynamic social and cultural change on market structures. The majority of their work is done with commercial firms to help them to identify consumer values which affect their markets.

The Synergy data was compiled using the Target Group Index from the British Market Research Bureau. Between April and June 1996, 5,198 nationally representative respondents aged between fifteen and 75 were randomly selected from its database. They filled in a self-administered questionnaire of over 800 questions, comprising demographic and value orientated questions. This is the *Insight '96* survey, part of an ongoing survey which started in 1973.

Demos' Serious Futures method

Demos' 'Serious Futures' methodology does not aim categorically to predict the future, but to create a picture of what likely scenarios might be through an examination of key variables and how they are likely to interact. The aim of this approach is to understand the possible future contexts for policy analysis. A detailed description of the method is available from Demos.